"Kent Eilers deeply loves the risen Christ and his students. These two loves shine through this winsome primer, which is full of creative energy, pedagogical skill, and spiritual wisdom."

— **Daniel J. Treier**
Wheaton College

"This is an incredibly important guide to the theological task that invites students — in kindness, gentleness, and love — into a world of theology that feels foreign and, perhaps, overwhelming. With the discernment and insight of a master teacher, Eilers shepherds students into the task of reading theology in wisdom. Building on years of experience in the classroom, Eilers understands the struggles students have with theological texts and the difficulty of helping them navigate these struggles well. Worshipful, prayerful, and full of insight, this book will captivate the imagination and cast a vision of a truly living encounter with the holy God."

— **Kyle Strobel**
Talbot School of Theology, Biola University

"Here is an opportunity to read theology wisely done. Enriched with art and prayer, and enlivened with questions and theology 'labs,' *Reading Theology Wisely* provides insightful and practical guidance for reading theology in ways that don't end with the reading. Kent Eilers leads his readers to connect theology with life and to be connected with God and others. Wise, indeed."

— **W. David Buschart**
Denver Seminary

Reading Theology Wisely

A Practical Introduction

Kent Eilers

Art by Chris Koelle

William B. Eerdmans Publishing Company
Grand Rapids, Michigan

Wm. B. Eerdmans Publishing Co.
4035 Park East Court SE, Grand Rapids, Michigan 49546
www.eerdmans.com

Published 2022
Printed in the United States of America

28 27 26 25 24 23 22 1 2 3 4 5 6 7

ISBN 978-0-8028-8178-6

Library of Congress Cataloging-in-Publication Data

A catalog record for this book is available from the Library of Congress.

For my students

Contents

Dear Reader

Dear Reader,

I wrote this book so that when you read theology you would come to see it as an activity of your Christian life – not separate from everything else you care about and do as a Christian.

This may seem obvious to some people, but the notion that reading and living faith go together is so often and so easily forgotten in the classroom. Assignments and grades and career preparation seem to be the main thing (I see it all the time among my students). The connection between vibrant faith and reading theology is also forgotten in many churches where theology is mistaken for dry intellectualism, and thus irrelevant for the Christian life or even harmful (I saw this on occasion as a pastor). Theology *can* sometimes appear lifeless or even dangerous, of course, so we should be kind to those who warn others off.

But what if reading theology wasn't mainly about grades or about our minds apart from life with God and with our neighbors? What if reading theology was about *expanding* our view of God, *deepening* our delight in his fellowship, moving us *closer* to our true selves in Christ, *seeing* our neighbors more as Jesus does, and *propelling* us into God's works of justice and mercy? And what if it could even *draw you closer* to other Christians, generating life-giving conversation rather than division? I wrote to help you read theology that way.

I also wrote so you wouldn't grieve. It seems like a strange thing to say, doesn't it? Grief was the way a student of mine once described her response to a first deep engagement with theology: "I have discovered a weird kind of grief lately," she said. "I feel sort of like I've been fed an easy, simplified version of Christianity my entire life and I was never let into the true depth. I feel grief over all the time I spent settling for so little awe and curiosity toward my Creator." She grieved that her view of God was too small for too long. She grieved missed windows for perceiving God's awe-inspiring beauty. She grieved hearing only faint and broken versions of Jesus's radical call to self-giving love.

So, let me help you read theology wisely. Let me show you how to see the written words of theology for what they really are: an invitation. Authors of theology have seen something of the risen Lord and what the world looks like in his light. To show and tell you the truth, they put their vision into words. Those words wait for you as an invitation: "Come and see."

Students reading this book may be wondering about now, "That's well and good, but will this book improve my grades?" Maybe. This book shows you what is going on when you read and write theology so you can see how reading theology *fits* in your Christian life. I'm a better student when I understand what I'm doing and why, and it's likely the same for you. You'll see that reading theology relates to many things you care about already, like loving God, worship, prayer, self-discovery, works of justice and mercy, speaking truth to power, and so on. Your grades may rise, but there's something better than better grades (dare I say): you may find yourself eager to read theology to deepen your love for God and increase your love for your neighbors. Why would we hope for less?

Maybe you're not reading this book as a student, but you suspected there must be more to theology than soul-deadening headiness. Will this book help you read theology toward a grander vision of God, a truer experience of your true self, and a more searing passion to love your neighbor? I hope so. Why would we hope for less?

I offer a few final remarks before you dive in. First, at the head of each chapter you'll find passages of Scripture paired with quotes from well-known architects. Together they hint at the direction of the chapter, but you may wonder, Why architects? Throughout the book I use our relationship to architectural spaces to visualize our relationship to written texts. Books, in ways similar to buildings, are spaces to *inhabit*. Second, you'll also find an original work of art at the head of each chapter. Chris Koelle is an amazing artist and a fantastic person. Our partnership has been a true collaboration and a privilege for me. I hope his art opens fresh avenues for your understanding and inspiration.

Christ's peace be with you,
Kent

1

Imagination for Reading

You are a chosen people, a royal priesthood, a holy nation, God's special possession.

— 1 Peter 2:9

Architecture is the thoughtful making of spaces.

— Louis Kahn[1]

"Why aren't they as excited about this as I am?" I often asked myself that question in my first year of teaching theology as a college professor. My students and I were there in the classroom huddled around some text. It was sometimes a book with the word "theology" on the cover, but not always. I worked hard to mix it up. One day we'd be studying a sermon, another day an ancient treatise, another day maybe a bit of poetry or an icon, and many days we worked our way through swaths of Scripture. With the Bible they perked up, but their reaction was noticeably different with anything called "theology."

I saw a younger version of myself in their eyes. As a college student, and later as a seminary student training to be a pastor, I had little interest in theology. I was passionate about studying Scripture . . . but not theology. Yet, somehow, between college and seminary and the start of my teaching career as a theologian, something changed. Now reading theology puts me on the edge of my seat. It fuels my love for God. It widens my view of God's world. It deepens my love for my neighbors. It enlivens my encounters with Scripture. It fosters rich conversations. Something changed, but what?

I can't identify a moment when this shift took place, but my perception of what happens – what's actually *going on* – when we read theology altered dramatically. My students and I looked at the same words on the page, but we clearly thought about what was happening in vastly different ways. You might say that, when it came to reading theology, my students and I had different "imaginations."

Imagination: What's Happening When You Read?

Your imagination and mine are constantly at work, fitting what we see and do into a larger whole, some unifying story. Using the word "imagination" this way is probably different from your normal use. We say that kids who play for hours in make-believe worlds have "great imaginations." Or we credit imagination with the power to transform an ordinary activity, as when a street sweeper manages the tedium of work by imagining herself reaping a field of swaying grain. Imagination has that sense, but it also has another. With the word "imagination," we also name the human capacity for *perceiving reality beyond the surface of things*. It's perception that takes place without having to consciously think about perceiving (this is how people who study such things use the word).[2] We just do it.

With imagination we make sense of our world. We fit together what's really happening at any moment. Even now, as I type these words, my imagination is at work. I don't mean that it helps me come up with creative ideas; rather, through my imagination I perceive the larger whole of my life within which this writing *fits*. My perception of the larger whole is undeniably shaped by my faith. I write as an adopted child of God, seeking to fulfill my calling as a member of Christ's kingdom under the power of the Holy Spirit. Imagination is a matter of perspective. Within my imagination – a distinctly and unapologetically Christian one – I have a sense of perspective that shapes my moment-by-moment perception of what is happening as I type these words. When we exercise our imagination in this sense, "we come to see what kind of world we actually inhabit and how we should act within it by glimpsing it from the right angle."[3]

The letter of 1 Peter is a good example of imagination at work. Peter's original readers were experiencing persecution because of their faith, and Christian readers have experienced persecution of various kinds ever since.[4] In every new instance the question arises, How do we make sense of suffering? Peter answers by drawing from the deep well of his Christian imagination. Suffering makes sense only when you see it in terms of God's larger story, of which you're a part. In other words, suffering has meaning only when you know *who* you are. And what is most essential about you, the Christian, is that you're caught up in the story of what God is doing through Jesus, which sometimes entails suffering. Naming the reader is Peter's first move at the outset of chapter 1: "To God's elect . . . chosen according to the foreknowledge of God the Father, through the sanctifying work of the Spirit, because of the obedience and the sprinkling of the blood of Jesus Christ" (1 Pet. 1:1–2).[5] Again in chapter 2 he writes, "You are a chosen people, a royal priesthood, a holy nation, God's special possession" (1 Pet. 2:9). That is who you are. Peter seems to be saying that to perceive our suffering rightly, we have to rightly perceive – *imagine* – our identity in Christ. He wants you to see that you are part of a larger story.

Consider this story by the French cultural theorist Étienne Wenger. Picture yourself approaching two stonecutters. You ask, "What are you doing?" and the stonecutters give very different answers. "One responds: 'I am cutting this stone into a perfectly square shape.' The other responds: 'I am building a cathedral.'"[6] Both answers are, in a certain sense, correct. And both stonecutters may be equally skilled when it comes to wielding a chisel. What, then, accounts for the difference? What limits one stonecutter to the task at hand but enables the other to "see" the unbuilt cathedral? The answer, of course, is imagination. The second stonecutter perceives that she is part of a greater story, a grander project; because of this, each hammer stroke transcends the block she happens to have in front of her.

The stonecutters in Wenger's tale are really no different from readers of theology. Picture yourself approaching a group of readers with theology books open. You ask them, "What are you doing?"

One responds, "I am mastering this material to ace my next test." Another, "I am trying to please my professor." The next, "I am trying not to disappoint my parents." Then the next, "I am preparing for ministry." And the last one says, "I'm being conformed to Christ by the Holy Spirit."

If you were asked, "What are you doing when you read theology?" how would you answer? What is happening when you read? What cathedral might you be helping to build?

Training Your Imagination

In this little book, I offer to train your imagination for reading theology. But here's the problem: I can't give you that in these few pages! Imagination is formed over long stretches of time, and it takes shape just as much through embodied actions as through ideas. What you do with the rest of your everyday life matters for your imagination just as much as what you do with your mind.

What I can do, however, as a fellow Christian, is try to winsomely portray this imagination for you, and (I hope) to write in such a way that it bubbles up onto the page. I can also suggest classroom-tested practices that help form this imagination. I call them "theology labs." You'll find a lab at the end of each chapter.

I did not set out to write a how-to book. I don't mean for this to be a book of tips, even though I often make practical suggestions. Instead, read the book as a *lens* for reading theology – an aid to *seeing* what is happening when you study theology as a Christian. I assume you're a

Christian, so the larger, grander story within which your reading fits is not the classroom but the journey of following Jesus.

The vision I offer, therefore, is a distinctly Christian one and theological from start to end. This is simply to say that I will show how reading theology fits *within* the Christian story, and I will do so by unapologetically drawing *from* the Christian story.[7] Seen this way, reading theology is not merely an academic exercise. The story of the class is not the larger story! The Christian reads theology – even when she's not aware of it – from within the story of her Christian life. I offer this account of imagination so that you *retain* that larger story when reading theology and remain open for what it could mean for you.

Could reading theology turn you toward God in astonished worship? Could it enliven your reading of Scripture? Could it move you toward your true self in Christ? Could it turn you toward your neighbors in self-giving love? Could it unmask your prejudices? Could it dethrone your idols? Should we hope for anything less?

Reading Theology is . . .

Reading theology is . . . what is it? We need a brief thesis. Of course, to keep this explanation from getting unwieldy, I can't say everything all at once. Yet we still need something, a shared point around which to wrap ideas and practices. Let's work with this:

Reading theology is a living encounter with an author's world of meaning, as fellow members of the church who are being conformed to Christ's image.

1. A living encounter . . .

Reading theology is a living encounter because reading is a bodily activity. What could having bodies mean for reading? First, reading engages more than our minds. We are not disembodied data processors. We are not walking brains or merely thinking things. God creates persons in bodies, living in time, space, and communities. Thus, we bring *all* that we are to reading – we have no other option. This is bodily life.

Second, reading reflects our perspectives. Because you are a living reader, some insights are plain to see from your particular bodily perspective, but others hide from view. You cannot climb outside your place in time, your family history, faith story, emotional makeup, or gender. You can learn to see from other perspectives, but you can never leave yours behind. Is this reason for lament? No, I don't believe so. Although our lives are stories that mix blessing and tragedy, joy and sorrow, hope and despair, life in bodies is the life God gives us and the life God promises to redeem.

As readers, we should not lament bodily life, but we should understand how it helps and hinders us. It helps by priming us to perceive elements of goodness, truth, and beauty in what we read. In this sense, our perspective is like a door that swings wide open. But it also hinders us, shutting us out from perceiving other elements of goodness, truth, and beauty – or, much more dangerously, preventing us from perceiving our blind spots, cherished falsehoods, and idols. We may read, for instance, from positions of privilege and power or from positions of poverty and vulnerability. We may not realize that such perspectives matter for reading, but they do.

Lest we forget, *writing* theology is also a bodily activity. It may seem too obvious to say, but we sometimes forget: written words don't drop from the sky. An author writes as an embodied person just as we read as embodied persons. I'm simply reminding you, dear reader, that reading theology involves you because the words on the page are an author's unfinished act of communication. Reading is an encounter. The author invites you to inhabit the space she created and encounter her world of meaning.[8] Will you accept the invitation?

2. . . . *with an author's world of meaning . . .*

An invitation awaits us in every written work. It's an invitation to encounter the author's world of meaning. All texts "project a world" and speak of a "possible way of orienting oneself within it," explains the literary theorist Paul Ricoeur.[9] First, they project or portray the world a certain way to the reader, even if not explicitly. Second, they suggest ways to live within that projected world, even if not explicitly.

Novels and news stories project worlds. Totalitarian governments know this, which is why they control the media and ban – or sometimes even burn – books that portray the world in ways contrary to their vision of things. Movies project worlds as well. Roy Anker describes the world-projecting power of film this way:

> No matter what the genre – from romance to science-fiction horror movie – the product is the same: a vast prolonged array of images and sounds that conjure up a vision of what a world looks and feels like as it moves along. Most moviemakers set out to convince viewers that the stories they etch with light "show" in some way what the world is, or what it could or should be. . . .
>
> The truth is that every film, whether a Bergman or a fairy tale, has its own version of the way the world is: garden or jungle, friendly or hostile, party or wake, full of delight or full of sadness, and so on.[10]

A textbook with the word "theology" on the cover or an ancient treatise on the humanity of Christ may seem far removed from novels and memorable films. Yet all project possible ways of seeing the world and then living in it.

What makes theology unique is the nature of its projected world. Works of theology unapologetically present a vision of the world *in God's light* and then invite the reader to live within that projected world. This framework raises the stakes. With theology, an author's world of meaning is as likely to disrupt our vision of God and the world as to confirm it. The disruption could be a gift of grace: uncovering our hidden prejudices, revealing our small view of God, reforming our worship, or widening our generosity toward the other. Such disruption can feel unsettling, to say the least, but not in a bad or harmful way. Theology concerns God and everything else in light of God, so the author's projected world meets us in an intensely personal way. It deals with all we hold most dear. "Open a book and a voice speaks," says the Pulitzer Prize–winning author Marilynne Robinson. "A *world*, more or less alien or welcoming, *emerges* to enrich a reader's store of hypotheses about how life is to be understood."[11] We know the power of fiction to paint a world for us, a possible way things could be. Does theology have the same power? Yes.

A work of theology invites the reader to see her world according to a specific vision. It's a vision shaped by God's self-revelation through Jesus the Messiah, the fulfillment of Israel's story, the hope of the world. In works of theology, the author's world of meaning is a vision of things *as they are illumined by God*. It's simultaneously a vision of God, a vision of you, a vision of your world, and a vision of your place in the world. Even when some of these are left unaddressed, they are still part of the vision. As a Christian vision, it refracts how the reader sees her world in very particular and potentially beautiful ways. What we need as readers is an imagination that enables us to see what is going on when we read so we can respond to the author's invitation.

But how do we get there? That is, how do we read theology toward living encounters that redemptively disrupt? The answer may surprise: we have to read *past* comprehension. We'll look at this more closely in chapters 5, 6, and 7, but I'll briefly explain myself here.

Making comprehension our goal hinders us from encountering the world of meaning an author projects. Don't get me wrong; comprehension is the basic requirement for every kind of reading, but it's just the start. Reading that encounters an author's world of meaning progresses through three movements: comprehension, understanding, and, finally, appropriation. First, we comprehend *what* a text says by grasping the meaning of key words, tracking the flow of sentences and paragraphs, discerning an author's use of sources, and so on. This is immensely important! Fail to comprehend the basic parts of written theology and we can't progress to the second movement: understanding. At the level of understanding, we discern what a work of theology is *about*.[12] Understanding theology entails perceiving not just what it says (the individual parts) but what it means as a whole. We can diligently work at comprehending all the bits, be the most dedicated student, and fail to understand what a work of theology is about. Works of theology are about their projected worlds: visions of God and everything in light of God. The third movement is appropriation.

Will we appropriate the vision? That is, once we see as the author sees, shaped by her vision of things in light of her knowledge of God, will we live "along the grain" of her vision – like sanding along the grain of a rough hunk of wood? Will we follow the patterns of that world? Will we march by its cadence? Will we make our home there?

Comprehension ——→ Understanding ——→ Appropriation

The best way I can describe this movement is with a spatial image: *inhabitation*. Reading as inhabitation is spatial. The two-dimensional nature of pages (or screens) gives the impression of a flat reality to be looked "at." However, the space between the covers has dimensions, even if that space is not formed by physical doors and walls. Think about the space within written works in terms of other spaces we occupy: we may enjoy a Sunday afternoon conversation in the space of an inviting home, a cathedral may strike us silent in wonder as it pulls our eyes toward heaven, or we might be assaulted in a space we thought was safe. When reading theology, we don't encounter merely a flat page. An author invites us to *inhabit* the space she created, so we can see as she sees.

Let me say two final things about the author's world of meaning. First, the author's voice is not the only voice we listen for. My friend Zen likens reading theology to hearing a sermon from a familiar pastor. We don't expect our pastor's words to carry the same authority as the Scriptures. Yet when we are at our best, we listen on the edge of our seat. Why? Put simply, we hope our pastor's voice isn't the only one in the room. We hope the Holy Spirit will speak as well, using our pastor's words to make us more like Jesus and more truly ourselves, more fully alive in every sense of the word (the process of "sanctification"). If we hope for the Spirit's activity through our pastor, why wouldn't we hope for the same when reading theology?[13]

Second, reading theology requires wisdom. The analogy of the sermon reminds us to be on guard for false projected worlds. For instance, some sermons interact with Scripture to promote misogyny and racism. In nineteenth-century America, some preachers justified slavery with Scripture, while others leveraged it to rally support for ending slavery. In the last century, the preaching of segregationist pastors fueled today's White Nationalist movement.[14] To discern such false projected worlds we need wisdom (the subject of chapter 7). False projected worlds reap destruction just as those based on right understanding draw us into the knowledge of God, enable us to see ourselves truly, and propel us toward our neighbors in self-giving love.

3. . . . as fellow members of the church . . .

For those of you who are Christian, it makes a difference that the author of whatever theology you read is a Christian as well. When this is so (and it *is* so for the vast majority of what you read as theology), then you encounter a space formed by a *brother* or *sister* in Christ.

Consider the relevance of this relationship for reading unfamiliar works of theology. The space created by the author's words may appear strange at first, and you might not immediately recognize its dimensions or understand its arrangement. "Why are the rooms this way," you may wonder, or "What kind of material is that wall made of?" Yet, if your sibling in Christ made the space for you, then you are more likely to regard it with a grateful eye and less likely to scorn the one who built it and run out the front door. The more you inhabit her space and encounter her world of meaning, the more you may find the Christian faith coming alive and growing more beautiful. Of course, you may just as easily grow uncomfortable the longer you remain, and you may even push back from the encounter, saying "I don't think I can make my home here." Whichever way you go, you cannot make the decision from the street. You have to live in the space for a while or risk misjudging your brother's or sister's projected world and what it could mean for you.

I realize it may take me some time to convince you, but entering and inhabiting the author's space is essential. Whichever way we respond to the author's invitation, our relationship to each other as adopted siblings in the family of God is the basis of our interaction as author and reader. An author may seem strange to me, and the space of her writing unfamiliar, but ultimately, she is *not a stranger*.

Could the author even become a friend? Just above I compared theological writing to a pastor's sermon, suggesting that we might approach theology with similar expectations of encountering the Spirit's work. Now I'm proposing a still more intimate relation. Aelred of Rievaulx, a twelfth-century English monk, says that spiritual friendships begin "from Christ, advance through Christ, and are perfected in Christ."[15] Such friendships are means through which God draws us to himself. Could we imagine our encounter with an author's world of meaning as an encounter among friends in the body of Christ?

4. . . . who are being conformed to Christ's image.

Reading theology is a living encounter with an author's world of meaning, as fellow members of the church who are being conformed to Christ's image. To say this another way, we read theology on *the path of being made more like Jesus*. The Holy Spirit does this with our cooperation over the long stretch of our life with God. We call the process "sanctification" (which means "being made holy"). Every Christian would accept that studying the Bible is a feature of sanctification, but many don't expect the same of reading theology. Why?

The Holy Spirit can take the words of another Christian – in the form of theology or otherwise – and use them to make us more like Jesus. God does this all throughout the Bible, using words from various people for his purposes. God even puts words into a donkey's mouth (Num. 22:28–30). How much more should we expect from a sibling in Christ when their words are used by the Holy Spirit?

Thus, Christians, throughout the history of Christianity and from every tradition of faith, have written theology to help others know God and everything in light of God. Reading theology is not the only way a Christian acquires this knowledge – certainly not! It is no substitute for reading Scripture, praying, receiving the sacraments, doing acts of mercy and service, hearing Christian testimony, and fellowshipping with the body of Christ. But if a work of theology is the work of a sibling in Christ (and I believe we approach it as such until proven otherwise), then through it the Holy Spirit can configure us to the Son's image and his self-giving love.

You may have guessed what I'm about to say. Reading theology is not altogether different from any other practice of the Christian life. All are understood according to our relation to God in Christ, and all receive their shape and character through the nature of God's incarnation in Christ. Said another way, the imagination needed to read theology is simply a subset, or smaller part, of the imagination we need to be faithful followers of Christ. Is loving your neighbor part of reading theology? Yes.[16] Is anticipating the work of the Holy Spirit part of reading theology? Yes. Is welcoming friends into hospitable space part of reading theology? Yes. On and on we could go.

We may not be cutting stones, but our imagination of the grander cathedral of faith will shape how we perceive what is happening as we read.

The Plan of the Book

The structure of this book follows my conviction that imaginations are formed by the beliefs *and* practices, ideas *and* habits, concepts *and* character traits by which we make sense of our lives in terms of a larger whole. While many of our educational habits train us to think about the supreme importance of the mind, how we habitually use our bodies and take part in communities just as significantly contributes to our imagination. Our imagination is formed through physical practices (things we do), and we perceive practices themselves as sensible and fitting by what we believe (things we hold true). The traffic runs both ways. We need to invest in both. For this reason, at the end of each chapter we reflect through prayers, engage with discussion questions, and experiment with practice-oriented theology labs – and then later in the book we consider character traits.

I built the approach of this book around an image. Several could have worked. Some writers fruitfully describe reading in terms of "eating" books or "conversing" with books, but my image is "inhabiting" books. Under the terms of this metaphor, an author projects a world of meaning. We enter this space through reading, even though our feet may not cross a physical threshold. And we have a choice: we can view the architectural space of a work of theology from the street, at a distance, or we can go through the door for an intimate encounter. We can make this space our home for a while. That's when reading theology gets interesting, involved, and risky. Moving from observation to inhabitation, we start seeing as the author sees.

Who Has Time *to Read Like This?*

Midway through the semester, I frequently meet with overwhelmed students. Sometimes it's the workload of college academics or balancing academic demands with all the other interesting and important things in their lives. Maybe you've been there, stretched thin and frustrated that your loyalties are divided between so many commitments and responsibilities. You can't give yourself *fully* to what you care about. "I'm in this class I love," a student tells me, "but I can't fully engage it because my plate is overflowing!"

I've been there, so I wouldn't be surprised if you were thinking, "Are you crazy? Reading this way – as inhabiting – demands more from me than I can offer during my busy semester. I don't have time or energy to read like this when I'm already stretched thin. It's not realistic!" (And your shoulders slump.) Do you resonate? I do.

As a theology professor, I frequently collide with limits of energy and time when reading theology. I want to read everything according to my Christian imagination – I really do! – but other commitments and responsibilities demand attention: interesting classes to teach, faculty meetings (which aren't nearly as interesting), and writing projects like this one, not to mention the joys of my family, friends, and church. I want to read everything according to the imagination I portray, but in my limitations I struggle.

Let's accept our limitations. Take a deep breath. Pause. Cut yourself some slack. Your experience is not unusual, and your frustration likely isn't caused by anything you're doing wrong. God makes us finite, limited creatures, and our limitations remind us to depend upon God in all things. We are not God, and that's *very good*! Of course, we could all be present in time more diligently and fruitfully. Our lives are littered with silly distractions, and we still have too little energy to allot everything our full devotion. Busy students and busy professors can't read every work of theology with the intentionality, investment, and heart they desire.

However, we can still *prepare* ourselves so that reading can become a living encounter – and maybe even surprise us when it does! Here are two ways to prepare.

1. Be willing to pray

Before you read, pray. You might pray that you'll be turned toward God in worship and toward your neighbor in love. You might pray that your hunger for justice and your will to pursue it would increase at the same rate. You might pray that God would prepare you to meet a fellow brother or sister in Christ. You might pray that God would sharpen your mind to discern truth from error. There are many ways to pray, but it's a good start to pray for God's activity in your life, a mind capable of discerning truth, and a spirit of hospitality. *Father, enable me to read toward you, toward the truth, and toward my neighbor.*

Theology can't survive without prayer. In the absence of prayer, it shifts from second-person dialogue (God as "you") to third-person description (God as "him"). Helmut Thielicke, a twentieth-century theologian, writes, "Consider that the first time someone spoke of God in the third person and therefore no longer *with* God but *about* God was the very moment when the question resounded, 'Did God really say?' (cf. Genesis 3:1). This fact ought to make us think."[17] He wants to make us a little surprised, even uncomfortable, by remembering that third-person language about God originated with the serpent who twisted God's words. He concludes with this: "A theological thought can breathe only in the atmosphere of dialogue with God."[18] He isn't saying theology shouldn't be rigorous or critical, in the sense of bringing all our intellectual capacities to bear. Nor is he saying that prayerful theology never includes description of God. Jesus did that all the time. Thielicke simply reminds us of something we consider more closely in the next chapter: the object of theology is *God*. We always study God as those already in relationship. Prayer is the ultimate dialogical context for reading theology: the dialogue between God and us.

Years ago, as I was beginning doctoral studies in theology, a mentor gave me good advice: Pray often, and mean it. Good advice. I've tried to follow it. Before you read theology, pray, and mean it.

2. *Be open to surprises (and sometimes discomfort)*

If we believe that the Spirit of God is drawing us into ever-deeper fellowship with the Father and the Son by conforming us to the image of Christ, then we shouldn't be surprised if the Spirit does so through the act of reading theology. The Spirit's activity is unpredictable and difficult to discern — it "blows wherever it pleases" (John 3:8). Without warning, the Spirit may grab us and make us what we could never become on our own.

When we are reading theology, the Spirit may reveal that our love for neighbors is paltry and thin. He may show us that God's world and our humanity are more significant than we ever realized. He may open up entirely new vistas, revealing that God is bigger, more interesting, more worthy of our worship, and quite simply more astonishing than we ever thought. And in case you weren't already prepared, theology will sometimes make us *uncomfortable* in the best of ways.

It will convict us, unravel us, and prompt us to think, feel, and act redemptively. This shouldn't surprise us, right? When reading Scripture, we expect the Spirit to cut us to the bone sometimes. And when our pastor preaches a sermon or a mentor speaks an uncomfortable truth that convicts us, we celebrate (or we should). So, we shouldn't be surprised when God uses good theology to make us redemptively uncomfortable.

For instance, in *The Cross and the Lynching Tree*, James Cone, a black theologian, unsettles me by pointing out the relationship between the cross of Jesus Christ and a part of American history I'd rather not think about: the lynching of African Americans. He writes,

> The lynching tree is a metaphor for white America's crucifixion of black people. It is the window that best reveals the religious meaning of the cross in our land. In this sense, black people are Christ figures, not because they wanted to suffer but because they had no choice. Just as Jesus had no choice in his journey to Calvary, so black people had no choice about being lynched. . . . Yet, God took the evil of the cross and the lynching tree and transformed them both into the triumphant beauty of the divine. If America has the courage to confront the great sin and ongoing legacy of white supremacy with repentance and reparation there is hope "beyond tragedy."[19]

Oh, that is difficult to read! As a white American, I'm ashamed of that part of our history. I don't want to look at it, but Cone won't let me look away. By forcing me to look at the relationship between the lynching of African Americans and the cross of Jesus, Cone expands both my theology of the cross and my sense of self. If Christians during the lynching era were blind to its darkness, to what am I blind?

Likewise, in *Burying White Privilege*, Miguel De La Torre, a theologian and activist, challenges American Christians not to keep the costly demands of the gospel *at arm's length* — tucked away in our heads and in our hearts, but just far enough away that little public action is required from our hands and feet. He writes,

> For Christianity in the United States, moral endeavor becomes a matter of speculating about what is ethical rather than rolling up our sleeves and bending the arc of the moral universe toward justice. While our current nationalist Christianity is the overall legitimized norm, it is nonetheless presented as a private matter. As long as Jesus remains

> a merely personal savior, Christianity can be tamed, demanding no action to implement Jesus's public teachings on how to live justly.[20]

I wish I could say otherwise, but I'm prone to tame the radical teachings of Jesus as De La Torre warns. It costs me less. And then I read theology like this, and it's like reading the prophet Amos, written to make me redemptively uncomfortable — to overturn my idols and propel me into the places where the kingdom of God expands with my Spirit-empowered presence. (An altogether different sort of discomfort arises when reading theology that is false. "Heresy" is the word used to describe it, and we will address it later in the book.[21])

I want to say very clearly that all this growth might indeed happen through reading Scripture, or through prayer, or through close companionship with mentors and pastors, or in worship, but it might also happen when studying theology! Karl Barth, one of the most influential theologians of the twentieth century, has this to say:

> A quite specific *astonishment* stands at the beginning of every theological perception, inquiry, and thought, in fact at the root of every theological word. . . . If such astonishment is lacking, the whole enterprise of even the best theologian would canker at the roots. On the other hand, as long as even a poor theologian is capable of astonishment, he is not lost to the fulfillment of his task. He remains serviceable as long as the possibility is left open that astonishment may seize him like an armed man.[22]

Seized by an armed man. When you read theology, prepare for surprises and sometimes discomfort. The Spirit of God may change you.

Why would we ever hope for less?

Prayer

Sanctifying God,
You are always at work in us:
opening our eyes,

bringing us to Life,
drawing us to Jesus,
expanding our vision,
making us our true selves,
turning us toward our neighbors.
Help us read theology as expectant disciples, ready to encounter siblings in Christ, and through them to be met by you, our sanctifying and surprising God. Amen.

Summary

Your imagination for reading will shape your vision of the larger story into which reading theology fits. According to the imagination described by this book, reading theology is a living encounter with an author's world of meaning, as fellow members of the church who are being conformed to Christ's image. We read as embodied persons (*a living encounter*). When reading, we inhabit a discourse space created by the author, who is also an embodied person (*author's world of meaning*). The author is our sibling in Christ (*a fellow member of Christ's body*). The Spirit of God may surprise us by configuring us to Jesus and his self-giving love as we read (*being conformed to Christ's image*). We should prepare for reading theology in two ways: be willing to pray and be open to surprises and sometimes discomfort.

Questions for Reflection and Discussion

1. If someone looked over your shoulder while you were reading theology and asked, "What are you doing?" how would you respond?
2. Who are the people most influential in your faith, and what would it take to let an author of theology become one of them?
3. When you read theology, what hinders you from being ready for surprises?

Theology Lab: Rummage for God

If today you hear his voice, do not harden your hearts.

– Psalm 95:7–8

I am pleased that you teach sacred theology to the brothers providing that, as is contained in the rule, you "do not extinguish the Spirit of prayer and devotion" during your study of this kind.

– St. Francis[23]

Rummaging for God is inspired by the ancient way of praying called "the prayer of examen." Tim Gallagher's description from his insightful guide *The Examen Prayer* captures its essence:

> Loving desire for communion of life with the God who loves us is [our] root desire. Prayer with Scripture, liturgical prayer, spiritual reading, and the other forms of prayer feed this desire. But the prayer of examen is the specific searching every day to find where God's love is active this day, where God is leading today, to discern what within me may be resisting that leading, and to discover the growth to which God is calling me tomorrow so that this deepest desire can be increasingly fulfilled. Nothing in the spiritual life can replace a prayer that seeks this awareness of God's daily leading in our lives.[24]

The examen prayer connects our desire for God with his activity throughout our day. Rummaging for God connects our desire for God with his activity as we study theology.

Too often we keep the joys and the struggles of theological study at arm's length from our dialogue with God. Yet God is active as we read and practice theology, *always* drawing us closer to Christ. Will we hear his voice as we read theology and then respond, moving toward God with our joys and our struggles? Or will we hold reading theology off to the side as an academic exercise and miss how God wishes to make us more like Jesus and pull us deeper into his mission? Rummaging for God is a way of praying that starts with our experience of reading theology and uses those experiences to move toward God in prayer.

Rummaging for God is dialogue: talking to God *and* listening.

First, the talking part involves telling God about your experiences when studying theology: what you are learning and what it means to you, what you are struggling with and how that feels. Telling God how you feel may seem strange at first. You might think, "Why should I tell God how I feel? Doesn't he already know?" Of course God knows, but it personalizes prayer. It changes prayer from saying what we think God wants to hear to real, honest, messy dialogue. Most of us need this desperately!

Second, rummaging for God is not only talking but *listening*. Dialogue always moves both ways. Having told God how much it means to you that he is leading you into deeper knowledge of him or how it feels to struggle with truths you can't fully comprehend, then you listen.

Listening for God is hard for most of us. This is so for many reasons, but one we don't like to talk about is this: listening confronts us with our fear that God doesn't exist. Tell God about that. This fear is not new to him. His Son, Jesus, was human in every way possible and that same Jesus now intercedes for you at the right hand of God the Father (Rom. 8:34). Trust Jesus to know perfectly how to handle your fear. He carried and redeemed every bit of your humanity — including your fear.

Examen Prayer (St. Ignatius, Spiritual Exercises*)*

Transition: Become aware of God's love.

Gratitude: Thank God for his gifts.

Petition: Ask God for his insight and strength as you pray.

Review: With God, review your day. Let God show you his activity. When did you experience *spiritual consolation* (loving attentiveness to God) or *spiritual desolation* (fearful anxiety)?

Forgiveness: When did you resist God's activity? Seek forgiveness.

Renewal: Ask God to bless your next steps.

Transition: Aware of God's love, end the examen.

Rummaging for God

Invitation: God of my deepest desires, show me your activity as I studied theology, and lead me toward you.

Dialogue with God about your insights.

What insights have you received? If nothing comes to mind, ask God to make you conscious of them.

Tell God what these insights mean to you.

Thank God for bringing them to you.

Listen: How does God want your life to change because of what you received?

Dialogue with God about Your Questions

What are your questions? If nothing comes to mind, ask God to make you conscious of them. Sometimes we suppress questions that unsettle us but that God wants to use.

Tell God how it feels to have these questions. Thank God for being present with you, even in your questions.

Ask God to lead you into understanding.

Listen: What does God want for you as questions remain?

2

Vision for Theology

Thomas said to him, "My Lord and my God!"

—John 20:28

Architecture reflects, materialises and eternalises ideas and images of ideal life.

—Juhani Pallasmaa[1]

UNLESS WE KNOW *WHAT* WE ARE READING, it is painfully hard to make any headway at all. This is true for every sort of reading: blog, tweet, pop-up ad, graphic novel, billboard, editorial, or legal brief. Reading theology is no exception. What exactly are we dealing with when we read theology?

Readers of theology sometimes struggle because they are familiar with similar-looking books from other academic disciplines. The words "psychology" and "biology" on the covers resemble "theology," but how similar are they really? You know what to expect from biology: facts about living things and guidance for how to study them. Does theology follow the same rules? What can you expect to learn from reading theology? What will reading theology expect from you?

In this chapter, we develop a vision for theology by considering four of its essential characteristics. Call it a "definition" if you must, but I'll avoid the word. I think you'll find the word "definition" feels inadequate after considering what theology entails.

CHAPTER 2

Theology: Four Essential Characteristics

When we break up the word "theology," we find two parts. The first, "theo-," comes from the word *theos*, which is Greek for "god." The second part of the word, "-logy," is short for the Greek word *logos*, which in this sense means "words about" or "study of." So, in the most basic, literal sense, theology is the study of God.[2] The study of anything takes time, and theology is no exception. There's a process that goes into it, and it involves a set of skills.

Theology shares at least this much in common with other forms of study (it's a process requiring skills). But as you give it a closer look, the similarities start breaking down. Studying God – who is *not* part of the physical order – is a different kind of activity from studying an oak tree or a robin or even a human. Biology deals with living things – we know that much – and psychology deals with the human mind and its functions. Biology and psychology concern objects in the physical world, but theology proposes to study God, an uncreated being.

Evidently, we need a thicker, more comprehensive vision of what theology is and does. The vision I offer you is informed by the basic faith commitments of those who practice theology and those who read it: Christians.[3] Theology is practiced by those on the pilgrimage of the Christian life, those adopted by God in Christ who are being conformed to his image through the work of the Holy Spirit. Theologians are those who pray truly, and those who pray truly are theologians, as the fourth-century monk Evagrius Ponticus said. For the Christian, therefore, practicing theology and reading it contribute to their sanctification. Theology is a graced practice of the Christian life. Thus, the four characteristics of this vision flow from the Christian imagination rather than from general notions about "study" or "academics." We look to the Christian confession of God to understand the knowledge of God.

The four characteristics informed by this Christian confession are not theology's only characteristics. They are, however, underappreciated by beginning students and often overlooked by experienced theologians who should know better. Sometimes we forget that theology is not an exclusively intellectual practice. Other times it slips our mind that theology is not tasked only, or even primarily, with providing ammunition for arguments over difficult and contentious questions. Laboring under this common misconception, a student once gleefully asked me on the first day of class, "What's your favorite theology debate?" We may perceive theology's range too narrowly, thinking that its focus rests exclusively on God and Jesus and the church. In each instance, our vision for what theology is and does is too small. None evokes a full, bright, and thick vision of theology. Theology certainly involves our wonderfully complex minds, but it entails *more* of us than rationality alone; theology does engage in debate over matters of truth, but it entails the truth of *ourselves* as well; theology's focus certainly rests on God, Jesus, and the church, but it also entails *everything* else – yes, everything.

Characteristic One: Theology's Object Is Unrelentingly Different

The first characteristic of theology is mindfulness of the unrelenting difference of God. This is perhaps the most underappreciated characteristic of theology and the most disastrous to forget. Our attention can rest on many objects in this world, but the triune God of the gospel as an object of study is fundamentally different from every other (we call this God's "ontological" difference).[4] This may seem obvious, but for some reason it's easy to overlook. Under fluorescent classroom lights or sitting at our favorite coffee house, we forget that God isn't like oak trees, robins, or humans.

"Who is like you, Lord God Almighty?" the psalmist asks (Ps. 89:8). Jeremiah answers: "No one is like you, Lord; you are great, and your name is mighty in power" (Jer. 10:6). As Christians engaged in theology, we direct our attention to an uncreated being who created all that is, sustains all that is, and heals the world of sin. We begin by acknowledging that everything and everyone is created and dependent upon God for existence and redemption.

One of the ways that Christian Scripture indicates God's unrelenting difference is the word "holiness." For example, the prophet Isaiah glimpses God in a vision, surrounded by heavenly beings (Isa. 6:1–5). They sing, "Holy, holy, holy is the Lord Almighty; the whole earth is full of his glory" (Isa. 6:3). God's holiness is, in part, the utter purity of God. Isaiah collapses in despair because he knows all about his sin and the sins of his people. We find a similar scene in John's vision where God's throne room resounds with the same song: "Holy, holy, holy is the Lord God Almighty, who was, and is, and is to come . . . you created all things, and by your will they were created and have their being" (Rev. 4:8, 11). Holiness names God's uniqueness, otherness, and, as theologians will often say, "transcendence." Clearly, theology is a form of study whose object is fundamentally different from mangroves or elephants! To remind us of this we use additional words like "uncreated," "infinite," and "eternal" to name God's *Godness*. Such words keep us vigilantly mindful of the irreducible, unrelenting difference between God and every other object we study.

What does God's radical otherness mean for theology? How is theology shaped by the holiness of God?

The difference between God and everything else was often on the mind of Karl Barth. He described theology as painting "a bird in flight, in contrast to a caged bird."[5] Can you imagine painting a bird as it flies? How much easier it would be to lock the bird in a cage before attempting to paint it. With a caged bird, I set the terms. I limit its movement; I control its space; it doesn't come and go as it pleases, but as I please.

Painting a dead bird is even easier. The nineteenth-century naturalist and painter John Audubon filled canvases with beautiful renderings of North American birds. To make his paintings in the most controlled environment, under his terms, Audubon shot the birds dead! Back in his studio, he positioned them as *he needed*. Then he painted how the dead birds would look if they were alive.

Which scenario best describes your perception of theology? Is it like painting a live bird, always on the move? Does it seem controlled and caged? Or beautiful but dead? Nothing about my early exposure to theology gave me the slightest impression that theology's object was living and active, wonderfully and terrifyingly *alive*. Theology's object felt like a butterfly pinned under glass. The results were lovely, like Audubon's birds, but it all felt lifeless.

Some theologians have suggested that it's better after all, safer, to limit theology's domain to the religious language of the church. Others say that we should not set our sights on the Living God but instead on the social practices and beliefs of those who acknowledge him. Safer, to be sure. But can we really look away from the one who has "life in himself" (John 5:26)? How can we turn our attention from the one at whose feet Thomas cries out, "My Lord and my God!" (John 20:28)? Theology's lens is wide enough to address or encompass the language and the practices of those who acknowledge God, but God himself – the wonderfully and terrifyingly alive God of the gospel – fills the frame. We must not look away: behold!

C. S. Lewis beautifully evokes this characteristic of theology in *Prince Caspian*, a story in his *Chronicles of Narnia* series. In one scene, a young girl named Lucy wakes in the night to what feels like a dream. She makes her way into a wood and finds a broad clearing filled with dancing trees. Moving into the swirl and swing of it, passed from one tree partner to the next, she enters a clearing at its center. There she sees, for the first time in this book, the great lion himself, Aslan. Lucy runs to him and buries her face in his mane. Then, looking at him up close, she startles and says, "Aslan, you're bigger." He answers, "That is because you're older, little one." What Aslan says next, dear reader, stands at the heart of studying the Living God. Aslan looks at Lucy and says, "Every year you grow, you will find me bigger."[6]

The Living God to whom we give attention in theology should grow larger in our view as we behold him. Tragically, I've seen the opposite occur far too often. God somehow shrinks, smaller and more like us by the year. It is heartbreaking, really, because with every passing year this *someone* should seem bigger, more remarkable, more astonishing, more the one to whom the seraphim cry, "Holy, holy, holy is the Lord God Almighty!" (Isa. 6:3).

As we practice theology, don't we find ourselves in a unique place? On one hand, we cannot entirely comprehend God; this is a long-standing and essential Christian teaching. God is beyond us — *for* us, of course, but always beyond us. On the other hand, we must speak of God and to God. In prayer, worship, proclamation, and in speaking truth to those in power, we speak of God and to God. This "both/and" is one of the most basic and enduring tensions of Christian theology. A. W. Tozer, the twentieth-century author and pastor, perfectly expresses this in prayer:

> Lord, how great is our dilemma! In Thy Presence silence best becomes us, but love inflames our hearts and constrains us to speak. Were we to hold our peace the stones would cry out; yet if we speak, what shall we say? Teach us to know that we cannot know, for the things of God knoweth no man, but the Spirit of God. Let faith support us where reason fails, and we shall think because we believe, not in order that we may believe. In Jesus' name. Amen.[7]

Characteristic Two: Theology's Object Is Its Agent

We begin theology as those who see ourselves as the only active agents in this practice.

You (Subject) ———→ God (Object)

But with theology we discover a surprising reversal. Unlike any other field of study, theology's object turns the tables on the one who studies and reverses the roles: the studier finds *herself* to be the one studied, revealed, undone, and renewed. Since God is theology's object, we can hardly expect to practice theology at a safe distance.

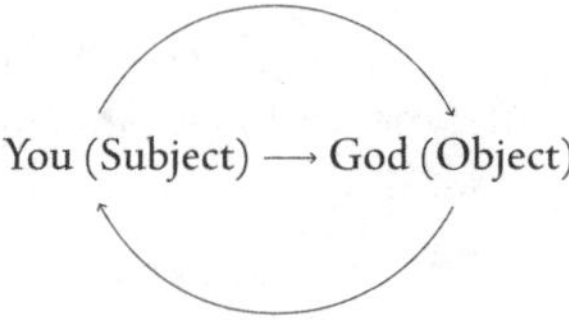

The tables are turned on us in theology for at least three reasons. First, Christian teaching about creation reminds us that we are, first and foremost, made by another. Because we are first "gifted" into existence, the sheer possibility of theology is open to us. Second, gaining anything from theology is possible only because *God reveals Godself* and not the other way around. Third, God reveals himself in order to redeem and renew. This is God's character. God may also judge, correct, and chasten, but he does so always in service to newness.

God turns the tables on the one who studies and becomes theology's active agent! We don't disappear from theology's pursuit – God honors the agency of the ones who pursue him – but we are surprised to discover that God was pursuing us all along. You may have thought that you initiated this study – or your professor initiated it for you – but God stands behind it and is active in it. One name for this discovery is *grace*: grace is entirely undeserved, and it awakens our response.[8] Hence, Mark McIntosh likens studying theology to venturing among crashing waves: "Perhaps [theologians] could be compared to children wading in the sea: studiously cautious, not intending to get wet, but magnificently upended by the vast, joyful rolling of the tide. The tide pulling at theologians is God, trying to get us to float, even swim, or at least admit we have no business floundering along on two feet in such a current."[9] Being "upended" by the waves is a wonderfully evocative image for God's activity in theology: unexpected, overwhelming, and joyful all at once.

The seventeenth-century painter Michelangelo Merisi da Caravaggio portrays this another way in *The Incredulity of St. Thomas*, which presents Thomas's interaction with Jesus after his resurrection (see the image on p. 194). As the Gospel of John records, Thomas would not believe until he saw and touched Jesus's wounds. Jesus invites him to do both: "Put your finger here; see my hands. Reach out your hand and put it into my side" (John 20:27). That is the scene Caravaggio portrays, but we should notice a difference. John doesn't say whether Thomas did touch Jesus, only that he saw and exclaimed, "My Lord and my God!" (John 20:28). Caravaggio imagines what happened in the seconds *after* Jesus's invitation, and by doing so he invites us into the scene.

What is it like to encounter the risen Jesus? In the painting, Jesus grips Thomas's arm, pulling his finger into the wound – notice the creased folds at Thomas's wrist under the pressure of Jesus's grip. It's as if Thomas thought he was ready but couldn't follow through – *it was all too much*. Jesus had to pull him in. Also notice how Caravaggio presents Thomas's response. Not unlike someone upended by the waves, Thomas grips his side to steady himself; his eyes bulge, and his brow furrows with intensity. Over Thomas's shoulder, two disciples look on in shock.

We wade into the ocean, only to have our feet knocked out by the waves; we seek Christ and find ourselves pulled into an experience that overwhelms – the object of theology is the Living God who turns out to be the real subject of our study all along. The *Living* God. He is not some inert idol of our own making (see Isa. 40), or some lucky-charm deity we hold in our temples and feed with our meager sacrifice (see Acts 17); nor is God a person like us, quick to revoke promises in the face of our frequent faithlessness (see Hosea 11).

God moves us forward through the study of theology so the one who encounters God may *never* be the same. We begin theology quite happy about our priorities and powers, thank you very much. My priorities. My powers. My plan. My budgets. My sense of self. All tidy. All my own. Then God turns the tables. The object of study becomes its active agent, and we discover that it was this way all along. God was working long before we ever knew he was, quietly, persistently, lovingly drawing us toward his presence and out of our shell of self-interest. We call this grace as well — God graciously breaking through our "self-enclosed worlds,"[10] turning us toward Life, toward our true selves, and toward our neighbors. One of my students modeled an attitude that embraces this gracious breaking when he prayed in class:

> Help me to see the orphan, the widow, the homosexual, the transgender, the woman, the person whose skin is a different color than mine, the foreigner. Help me to see everyone who appears different from me through the eyes of your Son, our Savior. Then help me to act on that vision.
>
> Oh Holy Trinity, you are One. You have reconciled all who turn to you by the sacrifice of your Son. Crucify our pride that we may love each other as you have loved us. In the name of the crucified and risen Savior, Jesus Christ, Amen.

Characteristic Three: Theology's Knowledge Changes Us

Theology concerns knowledge about God and ourselves. Because God is theology's object, and this unrelentingly unique God engages the one who studies, theology's knowledge involves our whole selves. Said another way, knowing God is intertwined with coming to know ourselves more fully and more truly.

According to the sixteenth-century pastor and theologian John Calvin, knowing about God and yourself is like two streams flowing into one another.[11] One stream leads to the other and vice versa. As your knowledge of God develops, you see yourself differently, and as you grow to know yourself in light of God, you realize your great need for God. It sounds like Isaiah 6, right? Catherine of Siena, a fourteenth-century Christian mystic, offers an image remarkably similar to Calvin's two streams. She likens theology to a mirror.

> In the gentle mirror of God she sees her own dignity: that through no merit of hers but by his creation she is the image of God. And in the mirror of God's goodness she sees as well her own unworthiness, the work of her own sin. For just as you can better see the blemish on your face when you look at yourself in the mirror, so the soul who in true self-knowledge rises up with desire to look at herself in the gentle mirror of God with the eye of understanding sees all the more clearly her own defects because of the purity she sees in him.[12]

Catherine and Calvin and many others know that theology's knowledge doesn't leave us unchanged. The Living God of the gospel is not inert or passive but actively pursues the one who studies. God draws his students into his presence and toward their true selves.

We might say that God is *interested* in the one who studies. Here is where the bird-in-flight analogy starts to break down. A flying bird is difficult to paint because it's moving, but it doesn't give much thought to the robin-studier. Yet, with the Living God, Scripture shows the opposite. The one who writes theology and the one who reads it are God's beloveds; they are the work of his hands and objects of his saving grace in and through his Son and Spirit. "For God so loved the world that he gave his one and only Son" (John 3:16). From the outset of reading theology, we're already involved with God. "While we were still sinners, Christ died for us" (Rom. 5:8). God delights in us so totally that he will not leave us as we are. "And we all, who with unveiled faces contemplate the Lord's glory, are being transformed into his image with ever-increasing glory, which comes from the Lord, who is the Spirit" (2 Cor. 3:18).

The God of the gospel seeks to upend our false notions of him, overturn our false self, destroy our idols, and renew our whole selves. Such renewal includes loosening our tight grip of control and moving us toward deeper faith. I know this personally.

Some suppose that academic theologians like me have theology under control – that we occupy tidy, uncluttered God-spaces, that we've plumbed the depths and have our questions answered, that we've chased away any tensions. That is not my story. Mystery is a regular feature of my engagement with theology.[13] Much remains outside the tight grip of my control, meaning that my theology is still unfinished (even as my desire for closure is unrelenting). For example, recently I found myself wrestling with God over psalms that celebrate the destruction of enemies. I knew a great deal about these biblical texts, but I could not find my way into them; I could not read them as my own prayers. As I wrestled with God, I found myself wanting theological closure. I wanted tension resolved, for things to fit into a tidy scheme. I received none of that. Instead, a prayer arose unbidden in the struggle: "Lord, after all the churnings and labor to find how it all fits – faith, You, the world, thoughts too high for me – just hold me and let me know that I'm yours, and that you know all about it, and that you love me, still. Amen."

The experience reminded me again that the object of theology, the Living God, is intensely interested in the one who studies; but God is interested in *all* of you – not just your brain. Our perception of theology is too often cerebral and excludes the other dimensions of being an embodied human. Partly to blame, I think, is the way that we misinterpret the great eleventh-century theologian St. Anselm's classic description of theology as "faith seeking understanding."[14]

The understanding about which Anselm speaks is not merely intellectual. In his day, theological understanding involved the life of the mind but also the state of the heart. We know this because the goal of practicing theology is not, for Anselm, intellectual mastery but the sense of delight that accompanies every personal encounter with the Truth.[15] The self-knowledge of theology is intensely *human* self-knowledge. We are thinking beings, yes, but just as much feeling, sensing, acting, and desiring creatures. Theology involves knowing yourself truly, which means you, the *human* studier, in all your human dimensions. We may wish it were not so. As an intellectual game, theology feels safer.

Theology isn't "safe" at all. We wade among the waves of the Holy One's self-revelation whose gracious presence never leaves us as we were; the Holy Spirit is always drawing us toward Life, toward our true self, and toward our neighbors. Walter Brueggemann wonderfully evokes this in his prayer "And Then You":

> We arrange our lives as best we can,
>   to keep your holiness at bay,
>   with our pieties,
>   our doctrines,
>   our liturgies,
>   our moralities,
>   our secret ideologies,
> Safe, virtuous, settled.
> And then you –
>   you and your dreams,
>   you and your visions,
>   you and your purposes,
>   you and your commands,
>   you and our neighbors.
> We find your holiness not at bay,
>   but probing, pervading,
>   insisting, demanding.
> And we yield, sometimes gladly,
>   sometimes resentfully,
>   sometimes late . . . or soon.
> We yield because you, beyond us, are our God.
>   We are your creatures met by your holiness,
>   by your holiness made our true selves.
>   And we yield. Amen.[16]

I sometimes seek the sense of control that comes from thinking I have the whole picture or from thinking in clever ways about subjects that are difficult to understand. God, on the other hand, is not interested in satisfying my desire for control. The Living God is interested in me; he *cares* for me.

Like so many others (perhaps you, dear reader?), I study theology in settings where I feel in control: classes that begin and end on cue in air-conditioned spaces. It seems that I can manage discomfort and observe my object at arm's length. And then God . . .

Characteristic Four: Theology's Knowledge Concerns Everything

"Wait," you're wondering. "You just said theology is about God and knowing yourself truly. How do you get from there to the idea that theology concerns *everything*?"

Think of it like this: God is the creator and sustainer of all that is, so nothing in all the cosmos is uninvolved with God. There is no self-created and self-sustaining bit tucked away somewhere. Therefore, when I direct my attention toward God in the study of theology, I am likewise directing my attention toward everything else *in light of* God. Willow trees. The family dog. Marriage. Education. Art. Politics. Economics. Everything.

To say this a bit more precisely, theology concerns everything *in its relation to* God. For this reason, the thirteenth-century theologian and Dominican friar Thomas Aquinas called theology "sacred science." "In sacred science all things are treated of under the aspect of God: either because they are God Himself or because they refer to God as their beginning and end."[17] The scope of theology includes God and livestock, rainforests, movies, careers, friendships, sex, race relations, climate change, immigration, and so on. Since everything has its beginning and end in God, theology concerns everything *as it relates to God.*

In worship services across every Christian tradition, there are moments when God's people remember that God's love for the world is not abstract and distant but present, personal, and all encompassing. One of those moments is congregational prayer.[18] People lead congregational prayers in many different ways, but their common denominator is this: a church acknowledges God's concern with everything by lifting requests to God about everything. Such prayers often include the environment as God's creation, injustice and international crises, national leaders and elections, local schools and poverty, missionaries and church leaders, congregations around the world and our local pastors, those suffering from various needs – physical, emotional, mental, relational, or economic. We pray in such a comprehensive and far-reaching way because we know – even if we aren't always conscious of it – that everything relates to God. As the very old hymn "The Lord Is King!" from Josiah Conder leads us to sing:

> Alike pervaded by his eye
> all parts of his dominion lie:
> this world of ours and worlds unseen,
> and thin the boundary between!

Everything has its beginning and end in God, so theology concerns everything as it relates to God.

A Thicker, Brighter, Fuller Vision

We started with a literal, rather thin vision: the study of God. This overly literal vision is brief and has directness in its favor. It also makes the object of study immediately clear: God. Theology's starting point is also important, which St. Augustine and later St. Anselm famously accentuated in their brief definitions: "faith seeking understanding."[19] Yet the four characteristics we just considered should inspire us to articulate a thicker, brighter, and fuller account of what theology is and does.

Our vision of theology must be full enough to remind us of its unique character without giving up brevity and directness. In the next few pages, building on Anselm and others, I offer you that vision. *Theology is faith seeking to know God and everything in light of God.* Let's look at it one clause at a time.

1. Faith seeking to know God . . .

"Faith seeking" reminds us that theology is an ongoing, responsive process. And "to know God" recalls us to theology's primary object. Anglican theologian John Webster expresses this priority in rich prose that compels us to slow down and reflect:

> Christian theology is a work of regenerate intelligence, awakened and illuminated by divine instruction to consider a twofold object. This object is, first, God in himself in the unsurpassable perfection of his inner being and work as Father, Son and Spirit and in his outer operations, and, second and by derivation, all other things relative to him.[20]

In other words, God first, then everything else in light of God. Whatever we might say about God's interaction with the world (his outer works) or the everyday things we care about as they relate to God (there are many), the theologian must first – diligently and cheerfully – give her attention to God's life in himself.

The first part of our description, "Faith seeking to know God," trains us to remember that the nature of God affects the practice of seeking to know God. In the previous section, we considered four ways that this happens. Yet there is another important implication of recognizing that God is the object of theology. I mentioned it in passing, and now we should look at it more closely: God can never be *comprehensively* and *exhaustively* known by human creatures, or else we are no longer talking about the Living God.

God cannot be exhaustively comprehended. This is an age-old Christian conviction, but we often do a terrible job of living as if it were true.[21] It was once common practice to distinguish between two kinds of theology. One kind is "archetypal" theology. This is God's knowledge of himself, which is perfect and complete, because it is knowledge *proper* to God. God's sort of knowledge. The second kind of theology is "ectypal": theology proper to human creatures. It is limited and incomplete because it is the knowledge of God fitting to creatures who are limited and incomplete.

As creatures, we never share the archetypal knowledge that is proper to God. No matter how hard we try, we remain creatures. But theology nonetheless proceeds as we seek to know God according to what is proper, or "fitting," to created, finite human beings. Our theology, therefore, remains an ongoing and responsive process characterized by a great deal of *humility*. Try thinking of this in terms of two dimensions of theological knowledge that are both true at the same time. On one hand, theology is possible because God wonderfully and graciously gives himself to be known. On the other hand, as theology proceeds, we discover our intellects, senses, and emotions struggling to keep up. Why? We are dealing with the Living God – not a spruce, carrot, or desk lamp! God is who God is, and vigilant awareness of this truth *fuels* our humility.[22] The fourth-century hymn writer St. Ephrem (known as "the Harp of the Spirit") beautifully expresses this idea:

> He clothed himself in our language, so that He might
> clothe us
> in His mode of life. He asked for our form and put this on,
> and then, as a father with his children,
> He spoke with our childish state.[23]

I tell my students as they wade into theology that they should expect deeper waters with every step. St. Gregory the Great, a sixth-century theologian and church leader, likens reading the Bible to swimming in a river. The middle is so deep that an elephant can swim, but it's shallow enough along the shores that a lamb can wade.[24] Theology is similar. Children like us wade along the shores of God's knowledge of himself without ever touching the depths of the middle.

When we read theology, we wade along the shore with our sibling in faith who wrote the work in hand. None of us will reach the deepest water. There lies God's knowledge of himself (archetypal theology). Yet we *can* wade deeper and even learn to swim with the help of those who know better than we do. Praise God! It is partial and incomplete to be sure, but it remains faith seeking to know God.

2. . . . and everything in light of God.

Theology concerns everything because everything stands in relation to God (or, as some would have it, "participates" in God).[25]

Let's tease out the meaning of this sentence: theology concerns everything because everything stands in relation to God. (1) God is the creator and sustainer of all that is. Everything has its origin in God and is sustained by God. (2) When we inquire into God, we are thus inquiring by association into everything else *in its relation to* God. In the same way, any inquiry into something other than God (tulips, black holes, neuroscience, and so on) pulls our attention toward that thing in its relation to God. The traffic runs both ways. So, whatever "it" is that we're attending to, that thing, or person, or whatever, is fundamentally and irreducibly related to God. To know "it" truly, whatever "it" may be, we must know it according to its relation to God.

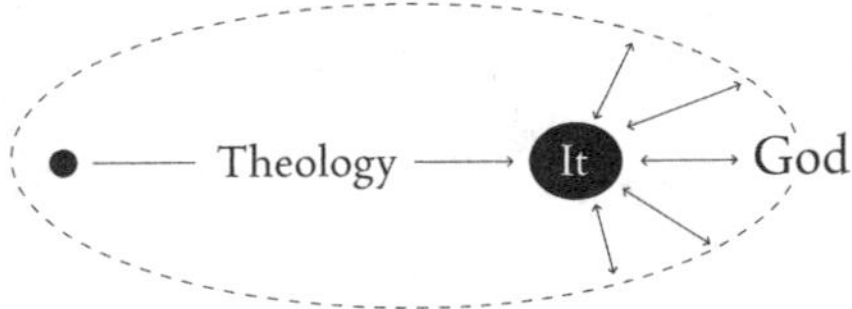

Does theology concern Christian beliefs? Of course, but it just as readily concerns worship, prayer, the prison system, technology, and entertainment – all in their relation to God.

If this is so, then what is God's relation to all things? A moment ago, I wrote that God is the creator and sustainer of all things (a basic and beautiful Christian conviction). Is there anything else we should say? Yes. Knowing things in their relation to God also has a redemptive dimension. All things are being restored, redeemed, reconciled, and healed by God. As Paul phrases it, God is reconciling "all things" to himself in Christ (Col. 1:20). In our realm of time and space –

"everything seen and not seen," as the Nicene Creed has it – God is restoring, healing, and renewing. We should not be surprised, then, to read Christ's words in Revelation when God's city comes to dwell with us: "I am making everything new!" (Rev. 21:5). Notice what he does *not* say. Christ does not say, "I am making all new things." Rather, he says, "I am making *everything* new." Every part of me and the whole cosmos of which I'm a part is right now swept up in God's redemptive work that will finally be complete at Christ's return!

Is theology an activity that should be separated from our daily stuff, cordoned off from the praise of God, or dedicated to maintaining tidy abstractions? No! Theology has everything to do with everyday life, because everything in everyday life relates to God and God's purpose to renew and restore all things in Christ.

Consider the Barmen Declaration (1934) in which Christians declared their resistance to the Nazi regime *in light of* their belief that Christ is Lord. The Barmen Declaration is very much a work of theology! In a similar way, Christians in South Africa used the Belhar Confession (1986) to declare their opposition to Apartheid. They did so *in light of* their belief in the reconciliatory character of the church. Public theology like this continues today. In 2016 Christians wrote the Ferguson Declaration to state their commitment to racial equality *in light of* Christian teaching about the divine image, Christ, the church, and a just society. Each of these statements reflects theology's concern with everything *in light of* God. William Ames, a seventeenth-century Puritan theologian, had something like this in mind when he defined theology as "the knowledge of how to live in the presence of God."[26]

Every second of my life unfolds in God's presence – every relationship, every occupation, every care and concern, every success and failure – and knowing God informs every bit of it.

No wonder theology was once considered the "queen of the sciences" (the phrase used during the Middle Ages as universities were being organized).[27] In this way of thinking, it is not that other sciences (or disciplines) are less important or meaningful than theology as ways to engage God's beautiful world. Rather, Christians engage the world through other forms of study *from the perspective of* — or through the lens of — their knowledge of God. Biology is a fine example. Biology may lead the Christian who studies it to worship God because her study of living things *is framed by* her knowledge that God is their creator (theology of creation). Biology may lead her to seek the flourishing and health of living things because her study *is framed by* her knowledge that God created her to steward his good world (theology of the divine image). When the health of the environment leads some to despair, the Christian who studies biology remains committed to its restoration because her study *is framed by* her knowledge that God will restore and perfect the created order (theology of last things, or eschatology). Every field of study blossoms with examples. No area of existence is left out. Theology concerns everything in light of the Living God.

I struggle with leaving you this tidily packaged vision. It would be a dreadful mistake if we let a "definition" tame the process of engaging the One who is untamable, unpredictable, and gloriously alive. If theology concerns the *Living* God, how could one vision represent him without obscuring facets and dimensions that other visions may better accentuate? We need a shared vision to move forward, but I'm stammering and stuttering as I offer you this one. Yes, this vision resonates with the deep texture of the Christian imagination, but it hardly sheds light on all I want you to see. In a similar way, yes, this vision is in harmony with many Christians before us, but it still risks settling the practice of theology into a predictable process, a tidy method.

And yet. Maybe my discomfort signals that we're on the right track. If the object of our study is the Living God (who, in fact, was the active agent all along), then isn't a bit of stammering and stuttering appropriate?

Can Only Christians Study Theology?

I wrote this book with Christian readers in mind, and I've cast reading within the journey of becoming like Jesus in the company of the church, but reading theology is *not* reserved for Christians.

Others will learn how those who follow the way of Jesus see the world, just as one who studies any religion will learn how ultimate beliefs shape an ultimate view of things. One can read theology simply to consider how Christians view existence and ultimate matters.[28] "Ah," the reader might say, "Now I see how a Christian imagination shapes their view of the world. I see how this would form a very particular vision of, well, everything." One can consider another community's vision of the world without embracing it.

This is all true, I believe, but something further must also be said. The one who studies theology is not the *only* agent involved. God is graciously active in all things before we believe, and this includes studying theology outside the community of faith ("in the shadow of the cathedral," we might say, or "on the church porch"). Before we turned in faith to Jesus as King, God was already at work toward us and in us; we call that activity *grace*. If it were not for God's grace, we could not turn to God, much less perceive our need for God: we are dead in our sins and our hearts are like stone (Eph. 2; Ezek. 36). Before we believe, the Spirit of God works mysteriously, quietly, down in the warp and woof of our life. That we waken to our need for life, that we see the darkness at all – these are the works of God we call *grace*.[29]

Could reading theology be a means through which the Spirit of God works graciously in the reader's intellect, consciousness, and emotion? Yes! God awakened Lydia's heart that she would believe the words of Paul (Acts 16:14). God enabled Peter to perceive the divine mission of Jesus (Matt. 16:16). God even spoke through a donkey that Balaam would hear (Num. 22:28–30). Should we hope and pray for anything less from the Gracious One toward those who study theology prior to believing?

Because of God's grace, we should invite our uncommitted friends to read theology with us: "Come with us as we cheerfully and humbly wade along the shores of God's self-knowledge." Our friends may try to keep a safe distance, to keep God's holiness at bay, but they might feel the current tugging at their ankles, awakening them to the relentless, loving pursuit of the Gracious One. Lord, may it be so.

Why would we ever hope for less?

Prayer

Living God,
You are not some dead thing,
some inert object,
some passive specimen for us to coolly observe
– safe, settled, in control.
You are the Living God,
the Holy One among us,
the table turner,
the idol destroyer
– "My Lord and My God!"
As we seek to know you and everything in light of you,
enlighten us,
even as you conceal yourself;
draw us near,
even as you unsettle our false certainties;
establish us,
even as you destroy our idols.
Help us read theology forever astonished and never the same.
Amen.

Summary

Theology is faith seeking to know God and everything in light of God. The object of theology is God, which has far-reaching implications for the practice of theology. Four characteristics are fundamental: (1) theology's object is unrelentingly *different* from every other; (2) theology's object turns out to be theology's *active subject*; (3) theology's knowledge involves our *selves*; (4) theology involves *everything*. People uncommitted to God can still read theology and, hopefully, encounter the Living God who is already seeking them.

Questions for Reflection and Discussion

1. How does your sense of theology prior to reading this chapter compare to the vision you found here?
2. Which of the four characteristics of theology seems most important? What would happen it were alive and well in your theology? Or in your church's theology?
3. What friends who do not follow Christ could you imagine reading theology with? What would that be like? What would it require of you?

Theology Lab: Pray to the Trinity

> *For through [Christ] we . . . have access to the Father by one Spirit.*
>
> — *Ephesians 2:18*

> *The very possibility of Christian contemplation is founded entirely on the doctrine of the Trinity.*
>
> — *Hans Urs von Balthasar*[30]

Theology is faith seeking to know God and everything in light of God. Yet we must not forget that the God we are seeking isn't some abstract notion of deity but the *triune God of the gospel.* We forget this so easily and to our great harm! This lab trains us through prayer to seek the triune God whom we know through Jesus Christ, who draws us into his life through the power of the Spirit.

By explicitly praying to God as triune, we form our imaginations to know him *as triune*. We cultivate our theological imagination so that when we seek to know God through theology (in all its different forms), we are seeking God according to the basic, fundamental, non-negotiable conviction of Christian teaching: God is Father, Son, and Spirit. The gloriously alive God – the one and only God – is triune.

The lab has two components. First, for one week, adopt the following two forms of prayer according to your normal rhythms of prayer and worship (for instance, fixed hour prayer, breath prayers, prayers before meals or studying Scripture, before sleeping, and so on). If you do not have a rhythm of prayer, set aside times to pray according to these forms. Of course, this all may be done individually or corporately.

The second component of the lab is a prayer journal. Throughout the week, record your experience of praying according to these explicitly trinitarian forms. What is it like? Do you love it? Why? Do you hate it? Why?

Form 1

Pray a prayer directed to each person of the Godhead (Father, Son, and Spirit) according to their revealed functions in the divine economy. This form of prayer does not deny the unity of God's action (i.e., all the persons of the Godhead act together in every divine action, what the early church fathers called *perichoresis*, or interpenetration). Rather, it addresses each according to their revealed actions: prayers regarding God's provision for us directed to the Father, prayers regarding our salvation to the Son, and prayers regarding sanctification to the Holy Spirit. There is a long tradition of this among Christians.

Here are a few samples you could use, or you could write your own after the pattern of these.

> Glory be to the Father, to the Son, and to the Holy Spirit;
> as it was in the beginning, is now, and will be forever, world without end. Amen.

> Father almighty, maker of heaven and earth:
> Set up your kingdom in our midst.
> Lord Jesus Christ, Son of the living God:
> Have mercy on me, a sinner.
> Holy Spirit, breath of the living God:
> Renew me and all the world.[31]

> Father, you have come to meet us as we return to you: Lord have mercy. Jesus, you died on the cross for our sins: Christ have mercy. Spirit, you give us life and peace: Lord have mercy, Amen.[32]

Form 2

Pray a prayer directed to the Father (Matt. 6:8–9) which explicitly recognizes the double mediation of Son and Spirit (Rom. 8:15, 8:34; Heb. 7:25).

Most collect prayers follow this form; it begins with the "address" to the Father and concludes with the "pleading" to Christ as our only mediator who lives with the Father in the unity of the Holy Spirit. You may compose and write prayers that follow this form, use prayers that you find elsewhere, or consider using something like the following:

> God the Father [insert your praise, petitions, etc.], through Jesus Christ our/my Lord, who lives and reigns with you in the unity of the Holy Spirit, world without end. Amen.

> God the Father [insert your praise, petition, etc.], through Jesus Christ our/my Lord, and according to the work of your Spirit, one God, now and forever. Amen.

Write and Pray Your Own Trinitarian Prayer

Having prayed according to different trinitarian forms throughout the week, write your own. Write something that resonates with your faith tradition. Write something that feels like *you.* Write something that trains and forms you every time you pray it to remember that you pray to the triune God: Father, Son, and Spirit. That is the God your faith seeks as you study theology.

3

Reading as Inhabitation

The secret things belong to the Lord *our God, but the things revealed belong to us and to our children forever, that we may follow all the words of this law.*

— *Deuteronomy 29:29*

It is not enough to see architecture; you must experience it. . . . You must dwell in the rooms, feel how they close about you, observe how you are naturally led from one to the other.

— *Steen Rasmussen*[1]

Let's take stock of what we have so far. We have a vision for reading theology: a living encounter with an author's world of meaning as fellow members of the church who are being conformed to Christ's image. We have a vision for theology: faith seeking to know God and everything in light of God. I hope it's becoming clear that theology transcends the small, air-conditioned spaces of our classrooms, involving all that we are and all that we care about.

Our next question is this: how do we read theology *toward* the living encounter that awaits us? Wanting it to be so will not be enough, though desire is a good start. We need a way to imagine the act of reading that helps us draw near enough to the author that we can see as she sees. The author's vision of God awaits us in written theology, but *we* may stand out of reach. Perhaps we don't want to consider the possibility of change; we stand apart from the author quite intentionally. Or, perhaps we simply don't have an image for reading that helps us draw near. To describe reading, I'll offer you a spatial image. It is drawn from our daily experience of entering and occupying spaces: inhabitation.

We live in homes. We worship in churches. We work in offices. We shop in malls. We cheer in stadiums. We study in schools. We stroll through museums, hands clasped behind our backs, gazing at the art. Every space invites its own kind of encounter, and reading is no different. Through words, grammar, and rhetoric, an author creates a space and invites us in. That space *is* the author's medium of communication, so to read is in a real sense to inhabit the space. As readers, we go "inside" to see as the author invites us to see.

This chapter has three parts. First, we contrast inhabitation with popular but unhelpful metaphors that distort the practice of reading theology. They run against the grain of deep Christian convictions. Second, we consider how inhabitation prepares us to approach theology in terms of its three worlds: *behind*, *of*, and *in front*. Third, we move from the abstract to the more concrete with examples from popular culture, my classroom, the ancient church, and Luke's Gospel.

Not Domination, Conquering, or Mastery

Not long ago I had lunch with a student to chat about our theology class. He was doing well overall but struggling with the readings. They were new to him and difficult. Another professor gave him this advice, which my student relayed to me: "Ransack your reading." I nearly choked! "How is the image of 'ransacking' helping you?" I asked (while trying to keep my food down). He gave a positive report. The metaphor prompted him to read proactively, to take something valuable from each reading, which is great. However, the image of ransacking a text is deeply problematic because it structures the reader's imagination to think of knowledge in terms of power and control. In my experience, the Christian imagination runs directly counter to this mindset.

"Ransacking" a reading may recall the notion of mastery, which is a concept I've taught for years. Mortimer Adler's exceptionally helpful *How to Read a Book* identifies two sorts of reading: for comprehension and for mastery. Reading for comprehension is needed for class; we read to know enough so that we might participate in a discussion or ask an intelligent question. Mastery, though, is something else – an earned ability to identify key terms and ideas, understand passages in their context, retrace the steps of an author's argument, and consider implications.

In academic settings, reading everything for mastery is impossible. Either you habitually leave some reading incomplete and feel like a failure, or you burn out, despair, and read nothing. I see this play out all the time, and I tell students about Adler's distinction only to relieve the pressure of reading everything for mastery, but I've come to realize that mastery and ransacking are easily confused. While mastery simply describes a level of comprehension that transcends comprehension, ransacking is a way of reading that runs against the grain of my Christian convictions about God. Instead of ransacking our readings like axe-wielding Vikings, the Christian imagination prompts us to inhabit them as *guests*. Rather than reading to take, we read to *receive*.

Let's put our Christian imagination to work and see what happens when we think about reading in terms of God. Immediately, we see that our view of God has power to shape how we think about what we know.

Christians believe God is uncreated and therefore not constrained by the limitations we know as creatures (we call this God's "transcendence"). What God is, how God is, and what God does are proper to God alone. The same is true for what God knows. What God knows and how God knows are proper to God *as God*. While human words carry us only so far in describing this, the following is a long-held standard: God's knowledge is perfect and complete. Still with me?

We are not God, thankfully, so anything we know about any thing is imperfect and incomplete. We saw the bearing of this principle on theology in the last chapter, and now we consider its relevance for reading theology. Whatever knowledge we gain in this life – great, small, profound, or petty – will be small in comparison to God's perfect and complete knowledge. A coffee mug, a neutron star, or your deepest self – God knows it completely and perfectly *as God*.

Thus, our knowledge *shares* partially and imperfectly in what God knows completely and perfectly. Given that relationship, our knowledge can always be understood as developing on a spectrum: moving either nearer God's knowledge or farther away.

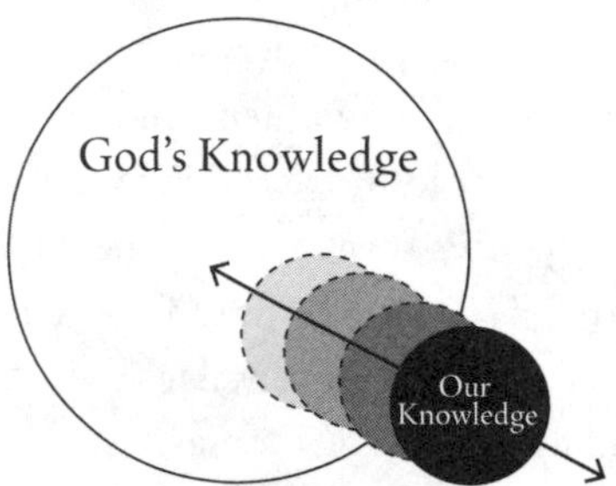

Musical metaphors also describe this relationship. Our knowledge is either becoming more harmonious ("consonant") with God's knowledge or more dissonant. Our ears know the difference: harmony puts us at rest while dissonance makes the hairs on our neck stand up. When we come to know something more truly, more as it really is, we move closer to harmony, alignment, or fit with what God already knows.

Spatial, architectural metaphors work especially well because they are three-dimensional and relational. We inhabit God's knowledge as guests, almost as if we were visiting the grand estate – a palace perhaps – of an impossibly wealthy relative. At first, everything feels strange and unfamiliar, like Harry Potter in his first days at Hogwarts Castle. The stairways moved, and the paintings talked. But with time and some effort, he learned to fit, to align himself with life in the castle. Now, when I put this in theological terms, see if you notice a key difference: we are guests of God's knowledge on his initiative. Do you see it? Sharing in God's knowledge is a gift. We call that *grace*.

Here is the relevance of all this for reading. Just as we are guests of God's knowledge, we are no less guests of an author's knowledge. An author writes to be understood, not conquered. To be inhabited, not dominated. We read theology to share an author's partial and imperfect knowledge of God – not to possess it. "Objects of knowledge so understood," theologian Paul Griffiths explains, "can be loved and contemplated, but they cannot be dominated" by ownership and possession.[2]

More importantly, authors can be *loved*. Reading as inhabitation prepares us to read as an act of friendship. In our pursuit of truth, or fear of being led astray, or desire to win arguments in our favorite theological debates, we forget Jesus's command: love God with everything you are and "love your neighbor as yourself" (Matt. 22:39). But it's impossible to read theology as an act of love when our mind is bent on ransacking and dominating. Sure, conquest images fuel active engagement, but they hinder us from loving an author as our neighbor. For the Christian, loving God and neighbor is the "first requirement for reading *any* text," writes Alan Jacobs.[3] Reading as love "requires that books and authors, however alien to the beliefs and practices of the Christian life, be understood and treated as neighbors."[4]

Let's be clear. Loving the author does not require us to wholeheartedly embrace her vision of God and everything in light of God (more on this later). Disagreement is still permitted. We need not live in the author's projected world to love her. Rather, love seeks to understand her, which requires proximity and patience. Love demands that we not hold her at arm's length, assuming we know all about her and her world of meaning from a distance. Love draws us near to understand. Is such proximity risky? Yes. Might it prompt change? Yes. Does it require wisdom? Yes.

I should summarize our progress thus far. What God knows completely, we know in part. What we know in part, God gives in the sense of being hospitable, of *opening his home*, so to speak, to the efforts of our minds. "The secret things belong to the LORD our God, but the things revealed belong to us and to our children forever, that we may follow all the words of this law" (Deut. 29:29). Ultimately, what God gives, he gives to conform our lives to Jesus. When we're conformed to Jesus, we are propelled into the creation-restoring, mercy-bringing, justice-establishing work of God's kingdom. Jesus said kingdom-people would be known by their willingness to love. To love an author means drawing near enough to see as she sees.

Wouldn't we want to read theology in such a way that we're ready for that?

Theology as Space

Much more could be said about the mindset we bring to reading, but we are starting to see why the metaphor of inhabitation helps us read theology in ways that resonate with a Christian imagination. Inhabitation leads us to view the author as a neighbor, not a stranger; it primes us to draw near the author's world of meaning; it reminds us not to dominate and possess but to participate and receive. When we become present to the reading in these ways, we read actively and in a spirit of love.

The metaphor of inhabitation also helps us read theology as *space*. To view it as space, rather than conversation, is the most realistic way to approach written theology. Honestly, I wish reading were a conversation between reader and author. I really do, but it's just not. To make the point, I'll condense some literary theory.[5]

Conversation requires people to share the same space or time. In each other's presence, we express ourselves in real time. I fluidly "point" to whatever we're talking about with words and gestures. Some of this holds when separated by space but not time. Conversing by phone, email, or text, I can question you in real time and you can respond through whatever means available to you, even if not verbally. However, in written communication, author and reader are separated by space *and* time. Bridging the distance requires something in between. Hence, the written word.

This dynamic is not unique to written communication. Painters bridge the gap through brushes and canvas, sculptors through chisel and stone. Authors use words to create spaces for the reader to enter and inhabit.

Written works are, therefore, like architectural spaces. They invite us to enter, inhabit, understand the meaning of the space, and then live accordingly. If a written work is about justice, its author writes in hope that you will live justly; if about compassion, that you will live generously, etc. Theology is no different. It invites the reader to inhabit its space, encounter its world of meaning, and then live accordingly.

Written works and architectural spaces both convey a vision of how life should be lived. Encountering that vision requires that we inhabit the space. As Alain de Botton explains,

> Buildings *speak*, and on topics which can be readily discerned. They speak of democracy or aristocracy, openness or arrogance, welcome or threat, a sympathy for the future or a hankering for the past. . . . In essence, what works of design and architecture talk to us about is the kind of life that would most appropriately unfold within and around them. They tell us of certain moods that they seek to encourage and sustain in their inhabitants. While keeping us warm and helping us in mechanical ways, they simultaneously hold out *an invitation for us to be specific sorts of people.*[6]

Written works also hold out invitations: inhabit this author's space, encounter her world of meaning, and then be (or become) a new kind of person. In short, reading invites change.

I'm doing this even now. These words, their order, my tone, the sources I employ, Chris's art – all of these elements are being carefully built into a building of words, an architectural communication space I invite you to enter, inhabit, and then live accordingly. The change I'm inviting concerns the act of reading, but there's more here. There's an invitation to see God in a certain way and to ask what your life would look like in light of this vision. These invitations are part of *my* world of meaning that *you* encounter as the reader.

All this comes naturally for us with stories, right? Writer Marilyn McEntyre beautifully tells how stories create spaces that change us.

> When we enter a story, we leave something behind. We suspend disbelief, abandon the social contract that normally binds us and adopt a new one. We consent to the terms of the story, navigate its spaces – architectural or agricultural – follow its pathways, peer through the windows it opens, and sometimes run into its walls. On occasion we lose ourselves or our bearings. We look for landmarks. We receive

> the writer's hospitality — or feel the discomfort of finding ourselves outsiders. . . . Once we have dwelt in a particular house of fiction, we hold within us a memory of its confinements and vistas. And that memory *furnishes and redesigns our interior spaces* where thought is born and nurtured.[7]

Haven't we read stories that affect us like that? Can we say the same about buildings? We may not initially think of buildings like stories, but the architect Juhani Pallasmaa says they function in a similar way: like a story, "an architectural space frames, halts, strengthens and focuses our thoughts."[8]

Does theology have the same kind of power to "furnish and redesign our interior spaces"? I would say so, yes. Works of theology encounter us differently, but the fundamental dynamic is the same: they invite *entry*, *inhabitation*, *understanding*, and then *change*. When we cross their thresholds and move through them, pursuing the understanding that comes after comprehension, we find ourselves — perhaps unexpectedly — at the author's shoulder, hearing her say, "See as I see."

Maybe this seems too obvious (forgive me if I belabor the point), but in my experience of walking alongside thousands of readers, none approach theology this way at first. We read stories for exciting encounters, and we remember buildings that inspired us to feel something. But not theology. Books of theology are perceived as hopelessly strange: mere words trapped on flat pages. Engaging them seems to require great feats of comprehension but little personal encounter. Sadly, that perception does no justice to their reality!

Pathways for Encounter: Theology's Three Worlds

How do we make our way toward the encounter that reading as inhabitation invites? We need an approach to reading that fosters intimacy and nearness, pathways *through* theological works that take us toward the author's world of meaning.

I suggest reading works of theology according to three distinct "worlds": the world *behind* the page, the world *of* the page, and the world *in front of* the page. Each is an essential pathway toward encountering an author's meaning, and all three are present in every work of theology. In fact, they are part of every book, painting, film, billboard, or building. They're present in every act of communication without exception. Want to encounter an author's world of meaning? These are your most basic pathways. I'll introduce them briefly here and in greater depth through the next four chapters.

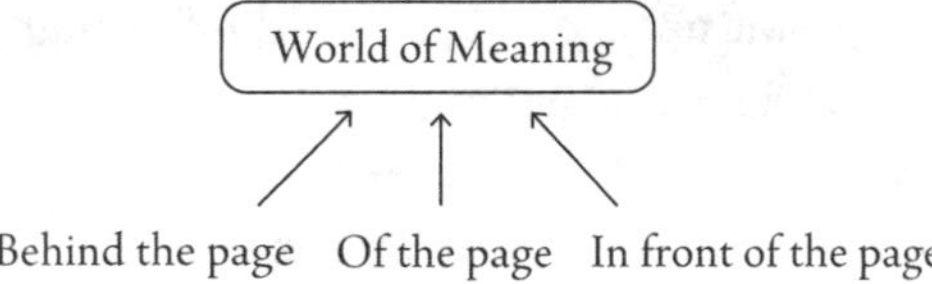

The World behind *the Page*

The world behind theology is the world of the author(s). Works of theology are built by living people in time and space. Words don't drop from the sky but are penned by *persons* with histories, personalities, and communities. In this sense, the author and her world stand "behind," or prior to, her written pages.

Traveling this pathway into the author's world, you discover the concerns of her day, the people who influenced her, and the experiences that shaped her. At first an author may not seem like a person to you, but as you travel along this pathway, she starts taking shape.

Perhaps you've found someone more like yourself than expected; or, you might be surprised at her differences. With either result, your sense for the author's words is gaining context and background.

A good example of how knowledge of an author's world illuminates what she creates is the central panel of the Weimar Altarpiece by the sixteenth-century painter Lucas Cranach the Younger (p. 195). Give it a quick glance and you know it's a painting of Jesus on the cross, but let your eyes linger for even a second, and you notice some interesting – even odd – features. First, the blood from Jesus's side flows in an unnatural direction, shooting across his body. Why paint it that way? Second, Mary is normally pictured at Jesus's side, collecting his blood, but here we find another Jesus. Why a second Jesus? Third, John the Baptist stands, as usual, at Jesus's other side, pointing – "Look, the Lamb of God who takes away the sin of the world" – but who are the other fellows? One holds the Bible and the other has Jesus's blood landing on his head. What is going on?

Not surprisingly, the unexpected parts of the painting grow clearer by looking at the world *behind* it. Cranach and his father were ardent supporters of the Protestant Reformation, and they laced their paintings with Reformation teachings. Thus, Mary is conspicuously absent from Jesus's side, precisely where artists up until Cranach depict her. Instead, Cranach paints another Jesus, a victorious one, to show that Jesus, *not* Mary, is the proper object of Christian devotion. Likewise, Jesus's blood shoots across his body, away from where you'd expect to see Mary, and onto the head of (get ready) Cranach's father. What's the message? God's blessing rested on his father's pro-Reformation art. Knowing that, can you guess who stands at his father's side, pointing at the Bible? That's none other than Martin Luther, the Reformation leader.

These features of the painting are left to point, like arrows, to Cranach's theology. But it's near impossible to follow the arrows without some knowledge of his setting, the world behind the canvas. The same is true for any work of written theology.

However, and this is critically important, no matter how long we spend behind the page (or the canvas), we will never encounter the author's world of meaning there. To be sure, our discoveries on this pathway will help us immensely: we may clarify an author's language or gain a sense for the communities in which her concerns and values were formed. All such gains serve our comprehension and understanding. But the author's world of meaning is *not* behind the page. Just as we could never understand Cranach's work without engaging the canvas itself, we have to move onto another pathway for inhabiting written theology: the world *of* the page.

The World of *the Page*

The world of theology is everything we find *on* the page, *in* the work itself. On this pathway we engage what the author left us: words, grammar, tone, rhetoric, the structure of the work itself, its form, and use of sources. Is it a system of doctrine, a treatise, a sermon, a commentary, or a poem? Does it involve Scripture, and if so, how is it interpreted? Is its tone aggressive or peaceful? All such questions concern the world of the page.

In this world, we consider the materials of theology and how the author used them to produce the work's effect. All that we gained about the author's world behind the page will be useful here, but traveling the pathway of the page focuses our attention on the space *itself*.

How do we travel this pathway? The author left us signs and gestures throughout the architecture of her writing. We focus there. We seek to comprehend a written work's form and shape, its terminology and grammar, and its style and rhetoric. Think of these architectural elements like "arrows" that are left by the author for us to follow.[9] When we follow the arrows well, we encounter the author's intended world of meaning; we see as she hoped we would see. However, if we follow the arrows poorly, we miss it. We see something else altogether, or only part of the picture.[10]

For example, consider the theological terms "transcendence" and "immanence" and think of them like arrows. An author will often use these terms to "point" toward her particular vision of God's relation to the world. To see as she sees, we must follow the arrows in the *right* direction. First, what do the terms mean? If we get that wrong, then right from the start we head in the wrong direction. We make no progress at all toward the author's vision. Second, how are the terms used? Comprehending the terms moves us across the threshold, we might say, and then discerning their *use* moves us nearer still. All such comprehensions, small or big, move us along the pathway nearer to encountering the author's world of meaning. We move closer to seeing as the author sees.

Painting follows the same rules, as we saw earlier with Cranach. All we find on the canvas is the world *of* the painting. The painter – who occupies the world behind the canvas – composed the various paints and textures, according to a particular style, and arranged them to evoke an image. We are left to discern the image.

Imagine yourself on an art museum tour. Your guide stands with you at your favorite masterpiece. What would you think if she said, "Notice the blue and red and that splash of yellow. See that smooth patch in the right corner and the rough swath in the middle? Take note of the swirly bits across the top and the wavy lines along the right. Good. Follow me to the next masterpiece, please." You know she failed in part (!) even if you're uncertain how to precisely describe the nature of the failure. The brush strokes, color choices, and their arrangements were arrows left by the painter for you to follow, and the tour guide failed to explain *where* they point. She failed to explain what the painting is *about*.

Let's apply these principles back to buildings. Crossing the threshold of a building, we enter the world *of* the space. Looking around, we recognize its materials: drywall, baseboard, cinderblock, paint. Good start. Still better, we comprehend how they're used: ceilings, walls, doorways, and so on. But we haven't yet understood how the building "speaks." What does the space *communicate*? Is it a hospital that speaks of healing? Is it a megachurch that speaks of efficiency? Is it a factory that speaks of productivity? Is it a tech headquarters that speaks of creativity? Is it a cathedral, with soaring arches pulling your eyes upward toward God in prayer, that speaks of grandeur?

Buildings, paintings, and works of theology are created to communicate. Through them their creators speak of something. A building isn't just a box, nor is a painting just a collection of colors, nor is a work of theology just an assemblage of words. Each invites inhabitation: enter, comprehend the arrows, and understand how the space invites you to see. Remember the words of Alain de Botton: "What works of design and architecture talk to us about is the kind of life that would most appropriately unfold within and around them."[11] We inhabit the space when we discern the kind of life that the work is "talking to us about." We comprehend the individual parts (the world *of*) in light of a work's context and creators (the world *behind*) so that we understand where it all points.

Comprehend the parts ⟶ *Understand* where they go

The World in Front of *the Page*

Have you wondered how three people can step into the same building and have three different responses? One feels immediately at peace, another claustrophobic, and another defensive. The world *behind* the space hasn't changed (its designer and builder), nor has the world *of* shifted (its layout of rooms and furniture, its colors and textures). Both remain the same. However, for each guest the world *in front of* the space changes. Each person brings their unique embodied presence, their own histories, settled habits, and sense of self. They inhabit the work differently; thus, the world in front of the space changes.

The world behind the page is static. The same is true for the world of the page. No matter who reads it, when they read it, or where they read it, the words, grammar, and rhetoric do not change. Like the architectural features of a building or the paints on a canvas, the arrows of a written work are fixed to the page, and the direction they point does not change. The world in front of the page, however, changes with every reading. This is the reader's world, *your* world. You stand in front of the page. You and the person next to you, and the reader a hundred years from now, will encounter the same projected world, the same invitation to live in a particular way. But the encounter will be different for each reader because each reader inhabits a different world in front of the page.

All writing, theology or otherwise, presumes a reader. As the twentieth-century novelist Flannery O'Connor says, "You may write for the joy of it, but the act of writing is not complete in itself. It has its end in its audience."[12] The audience of a written work changes from one reader to the next; therefore, the author's projected world is looked upon by people with different histories, communities, and expectations. The author's invitation to see as she sees doesn't change, nor does the written space she's created for you to inhabit. But every new reader brings a new world in front of the page.

Buildings, paintings, and works of theology point toward a world of meaning the beholder is meant to appropriate. To appropriate, in this context, means to adopt, accept, or live within. The encounter itself does not happen *in* the world of the work. You can't climb into a wall, onto a canvas, or between the words on the page. Your encounter happens in front of a theological work as *you*, the reader, see as the author invites you to see. The world in front is the space *you* occupy in the building, the position *you* occupy before the painting, and the conscious interaction *you* bring to the act of reading.

With theology, in front of the page we encounter – as our unique selves, in our time and place – the vision of the world in light of God that the author created this discourse space to offer us. The author invites, "See as I see, and live along the grain of this projected world." The way de Botton speaks of buildings is once again helpful: buildings "speak of democracy or aristocracy, openness or arrogance, welcome or threat, a sympathy for the future or a hankering for the past. . . . While keeping us warm and helping us in mechanical ways, they simultaneously hold out an invitation for us to be specific sorts of people."[13] Democracy, openness, or threat are worlds of meaning that encounter us and simultaneously invite us to take up residence (be specific sorts of people). Written works also "speak of a possible world," as Ricoeur phrases it, "and of a possible way of orienting oneself within it."[14]

Theology invites you, dear reader, to inhabit its world.

Theology's Three Worlds

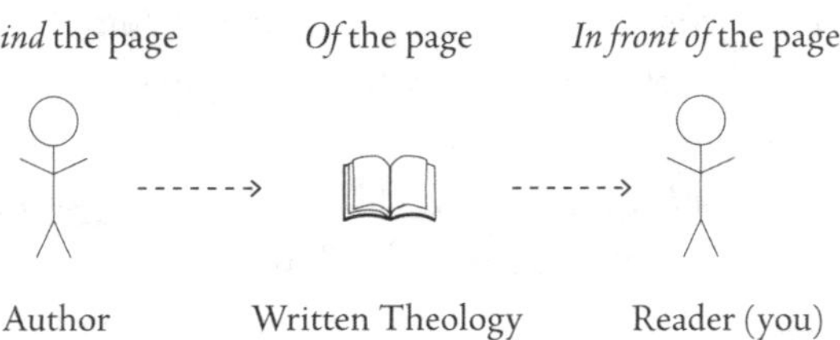

Real-World Examples

Toy Story 3

Years ago I watched *Toy Story 3* in the theater with my wife and two daughters and had an unexpected response at the end. More on that in a moment. First, let's consider its three worlds.

The world *behind Toy Story 3* includes its director and writers, its producers and artists, its editors and soundtrack composers, its production company, and so on. It also includes the time and culture in which it was produced and all the personal histories of those involved. Those people in that time and place are the world behind the screen. It's a richly textured world.

We find the world *of* the movie on the screen. It's the colors and characters, plot and music, dialogue and silences and how they're all arranged to create an effect. The movie conjures, as Anker says all movies do, "a vision of what a world looks like as it moves along . . . what the world is, or what it could or should be."[15]

When I watched *Toy Story 3* with my family, there were four different responses (or worlds) *in front of* the screen: me, my wife, my daughter Hannah, and my other daughter Abby. Though we encountered the same world of meaning, the encounter was unique for each of us. I found myself, at the end of the movie, the only one crying. *Me*, not my kids or my wife; I totally didn't see that coming.

My family and I encountered the same world of the film. We saw the same images, heard the same soundtrack, and followed the same plot. Yet when I encountered that world of meaning, something about *me* produced a deep emotional reaction. It's too complex to entirely tease apart, but I suspect the following. In *Toy Story 3*'s world, friendship and family are treasured, sacrifice prevails over selfishness, and love triumphs over fear. Was it that I followed these arrows better than my family and thus encountered the filmmaker's world more fully? Perhaps. Or, more likely I think, it was the uniqueness of my particular encounter with *Toy Story 3* – my experiences, emotional profile, faith journey, the sort of week I was having – that caused me to encounter the film's world in such a way that tears flowed.

Year after year, I see the same differences among readers of theology. One reads with a yawn, another with puzzlement, and another with astonishment. It prompts some to embark on new career paths, others to reform their entire way of imagining the world, and others to shrug their shoulders, "Meh." This no longer surprises me because I know the world in front of theology is inhabited by *living, embodied persons*. Each is unique.

Prince Caspian

In the last chapter, I recounted a scene from C. S. Lewis's book *Prince Caspian* in which Lucy meets Aslan among the dancing trees. What are its three worlds?

The world behind the page is C. S. Lewis's world. Lewis was an English literature professor and a very talented theologian. He wrote *The Chronicles of Narnia* as children's stories, but they are very much theology at the same time. The world of Narnia is a narrative experiment in considering what it would be like if God were to encounter such a world as Narnia. What would it be like for Jesus to be God in Narnia

(Aslan), and what would we notice that we've grown too accustomed to in our own world?

Consider the scene I recounted in the last chapter. The world of the page includes the characters of Lucy, the dancing trees, and Aslan. It also includes the plot up to this point, including the other books that precede *Prince Caspian*. Taken together, these elements of the scene project a world in which Aslan is beyond the comprehension of young Lucy and Lucy's sense of him grows larger every year. Lewis worked from within a Christian imagination; thus, the scene evokes basic Christian teaching about God (even if not perceived as such by the reader). God, like Aslan, is beyond our total comprehension; life with God in fellowship with Jesus should lead to a progressively larger sense of God's majesty; in short, God gets bigger in our view every year we grow older.

The world in front of the scene is me, and because I constantly change, my *response* to Lewis's projected world changes with each reading. I inhabit the space differently as I change. I'll be specific. I read *Prince Caspian* for the first time when I was twenty-two, lying in a sleeping bag in Joshua Tree National Park. I had no memorable response then. But when I read it again, as a father, snuggling with my daughters, I was deeply moved. I wept because I desperately want my children to experience God as Lucy does (I cry often when I'm healthy). I sometimes read the story to my theology students when I feel the moment is right, and I often get misty-eyed (like I said, I cry often). They aren't my kids, but I care about them. I don't want for them what I've seen among so many Christians: a small god getting smaller by the year.

On Holy Images

Toy Story 3 and Narnia might feel distant from the kinds of theology you're reading. *On Holy Images* (c. 730), however, is a theological treatise written by John of Damascus in which we find the same three worlds.

The world *behind* the page is particularly important given the historical distance between us and John. In the eighth century, a controversy raged about the use of icons (paintings of Christ, saints, and biblical stories). The issue was this: whenever we represent Christ visually, we can only represent his human nature. The human nature is what we see in the face of Jesus. Yet Christ is both human *and* God. Icons of Jesus, therefore, only represent him partially, and this was a big problem for some.

Those against icons ("iconoclasts") argued that icons are harmful because they don't present Christ truly as human and God.[16] Those who favored icons ("iconophiles") reasoned from the incarnation in the other direction. They contended that when Christ took on flesh — "made like us in all respects" (Heb. 2) — God transformed not just humanity but *all* physical reality. Through Christ, God made physical things capable of mediating God's presence to us, particularly, though not exclusively, through icons. John of Damascus was the primary spokesperson for the position of the pro-icon Christians.

When we turn our attention to the world *of* the page, we consider *On Holy Images* itself. In one of John's arguments, he reasons theologically by thinking about icons in terms of the cosmic reach of Christ's incarnation. Everyone involved accepted the truth of the incarnation: the Son of God became truly and authentically human in order to redeem humanity totally. Jesus took on flesh to redeem us *all the way down into the depths of our humanity.* From this universally shared conviction, John of Damascus reasons that the full, true, authentic humanity of Jesus should also shape how we think about icons. He writes,

> When God is seen clothed in flesh, and conversing with men [as someone viewing an icon would see Jesus], I make an image of the God whom I see. I do not worship matter, I worship the God of matter, who became matter for my sake, and deigned to inhabit matter, who worked out my salvation through matter. I will not cease from honouring that matter which works my salvation. I venerate it, though not as God.[17]

Because God "inhabited matter" for our sake, John reasons, God made physical things – like icons – capable of good use in Christian worship. It's not idolatry, he argues, because the icon isn't itself God. The physical world of matter has itself been affected and changed so totally through Christ's incarnation that things of matter are capable of use in Christian worship. This theological vision is found in the world *of* the page. Through comprehending the terms, parsing the grammar, and situating it all in the context of the eighth-century debate, we move toward encountering the world John projects.

What kind of world does *On Holy Images* project? Certainly, it includes much regarding icons and Christ, but is the work actually about something more encompassing? Yes. When we stand next to John, we're invited to see a world in which the incarnation transforms *every* physical thing. All matter has potential to mediate God's activity, according to this projected world. The basic situation of created reality is not resistance to grace but receptivity.[18]

On Holy Images invites the reader not only to see icons in a particular way but to see the cosmos in a particular way and to live accordingly. John's treatise shapes a vision that directs your basic perception of God's relationship to every physical thing. To put it differently, on the metaphor of wood, the projected world of *On Holy Images* has a "grain" to it. Those who accept it will live *along* that grain; they will follow its basic, inherent direction. Eastern Christianity has been living along that grain for fifteen hundred years.[19]

The Gospel of Luke

Each of the four gospels is a Holy Spirit–inspired witness to the life of Christ. They are trustworthy, and they are authoritative, *and* they are works of theology. As written works, each gospel projects a vision of the world as it really is in light of the coming of God's promised Messiah. We can trust this projected world; we can leap across its threshold and confidently live along its grain! Leaving aside the world behind the page, what kind of world does the Gospel of Luke project and what could it mean to live along its grain?

The space of Luke's Gospel repeatedly brings the reader face to face with people on the margins. More than any other gospel, Luke looks intently at Jesus's countercultural interactions with women, his physical contacts with the sick and diseased and demon-possessed – that scandalized many – and his behavior around sinners who were excluded from community. Luke's Gospel is "aimed at the world of those who do not belong, be they Jews, Gentiles, or whoever" and is "out to question . . . the way we draw our boundaries."[20] Luke's theology is not distinct from Jesus (of course); he did not make it up. Rather, Luke frames the truth of Jesus in unique ways that draw distinct features of Jesus's life and witness to the surface.

How does the Gospel of Luke invite us to see in *our* particular world in front?[21] Luke's Gospel projects a world of overturned boundaries, where our perception of those we consider outsiders is reframed according to the truth of Jesus. Through Jesus, God brings salvation to *all* people by breaking down the barriers that divide us: class, race, gender, sexuality, religious affiliation, or political alliance.[22]

Jesus breaks down our patterns of calculating human worth – who matters and who doesn't and therefore who gets near me and who I keep at arm's length.[23] Luke draws this to the surface in his gospel in ways unique from the others by tracing the patterns of Jesus's love for those at the margins: women, the poor, sinners, gentiles, the unclean, children. It's not that Jesus is present with them in some special way that he isn't present with others (though I understand why some say so). Rather, the *way* Jesus is present with them reveals the real nature of God's holiness, uniqueness, and otherness. Jesus shows what God's transcendence looks like as it walks along.

> God's transcendence is in some sense present in and with those who do not have a voice, in and with those without power to affect their world, in and with those believed to have *lost* any right they might have had in the world. God is not with them because they are natu-

> rally virtuous, or because they are martyrs; he is simply there *in* the fact that they are "left over" when the social and moral score is added up by the managers of social and moral behaviour.[24]

Luke's Gospel puts the question to us (in our particular world in front of this text): Will *we* live along this grain?

When you stand at Luke's shoulder, where do you stand? Who are those you perceive as outsiders? Who are those at the margins? Who are those you keep at arm's length on account of their status and standing? When we take the practice of reading the Gospel of Luke as inhabitation, we must draw near enough to it that these questions actually encounter us.

Prayer

Knowing God,
We know less than we'd like about so much:
    our world — why these fires and floods?
    our politics — why these wars and walls?
    our inner lives — why these pains and fears?
    our future — how will it all be well?
But you know as only you can know.
    You know as God.
Be hospitable with us as we read theology.
    Invite us to share
        partially and imperfectly
    in what you know
        perfectly and completely,
    that we would follow you wherever you lead, even as we know less than we'd like. Amen.

Summary

Reading as inhabitation is reading toward intimacy and love rather than domination and mastery. It moves us into the space of theological writing as we would inhabit a physical space. When inhabiting the space, we encounter the author's world of meaning, seeing as they see. Every work of theology has three worlds: the world behind the page, the world of the page, and the world in front of the page. The world *behind* is the author's world; the world *of* is the language, grammar, rhetoric, and so on that form the space of the work itself and projects the author's vision of God and everything in light of God; the world *in front* is the reader's unique, embodied presence in which they encounter the author's vision. The three worlds together open the space for reading as inhabitation.

Questions for Reflection and Discussion

1. Can you remember when a story changed your life? What would it take for reading theology to have the same kind of effect?
2. Ponder the diagram on page 52: How does it help you understand the process of reading theology as a Christian?
3. What would it mean for you to love an author as your neighbor? What would hinder you or help you?

Theology Lab: Interpret a Movie

> *Do not conform to the pattern of this world, but be transformed by the renewing of your mind.*
>
> — *Romans 12:2*

> *Christians cannot afford to continue sleepwalking their way through contemporary culture, letting their lives, and especially*

> *their imaginations, become conformed to culturally devised myths, each of which promises more than it can deliver.*
>
> — *Kevin Vanhoozer*[25]

Reading theology according to its three worlds (behind, of, in front of) is challenging at first. We know less about theological readings than other kinds of texts, like movies, but we can leverage that to our advantage. Interpreting a movie according to its three worlds trains us to inhabit theology according to the same method.[26]

Often movie discussions devolve into opinions and hunches: "I think the movie was about X," one person passionately says, while another with no less passion says, "But I think it's about Y!" Or the people having the conversation lack any useful language to describe what they experienced: "I liked it," one says, but when asked to explain they can only muster, "I don't know. I just did."

For this lab, gather a group of friends to watch the movie you want to interpret. Watch it together, then spend a few days following the steps below and writing up some notes. Get back together and discuss your findings. I think you'll find that the conversation goes much better than before, and you'll discover that reading theology according to the three worlds becomes more natural.

Part 1: Give a Thick Description of the Movie

Before you try to interpret the film, simply describe it. Seek to understand the movie according to its three worlds.

Interpret the World behind *the Screen*

Explore the world behind the screen by learning about the creators of the movie and their context. A little internet research will often uncover information about the director, screenwriters, and the concerns of their day. Why did they produce this movie? What can you discern about their vision of life, their values, or the issues that concern them? What was going on in their time that may have influenced their creation? (Sometimes they tell you.)

Interpret the World on *the Screen*

The plot, characters, soundtrack, lighting, and so on constitute the world of the screen. All these are the elements left for you, the viewer. Through them the filmmakers communicate a vision of the way the world is. "No matter what the genre," Roy Anker writes,

> from romance to science-fiction horror movie – the product is the same: a vast prolonged array of images and sounds that conjure up a vision of what a world looks and feels like as it moves along. Most moviemakers set out to convince viewers that the stories they etch with light "show" in some way what the world is, or what it could or should be. . . .
>
> The truth is that every film, whether a Bergman or a fairy tale, has its own version of the way the world is: garden or jungle, friendly or hostile, party or wake, full of delight or full of sadness, and so on.[27]

What version of the world does this movie present, and what are the elements *on the screen* that accomplish this? Is it the plot – how? Is it character development – how? Is it the soundtrack – how?

Don't worry too much whether *you* would see the world this way. Focus on giving a thick, careful interpretation of what you believe the filmmakers are trying to show you.

Interpret the World in Front of *the Screen*

What kind of persons do we become when we accept this movie's invitation to dwell in its projected world? What values would I hold dear? About what would I be concerned? How would I understand myself as a human being in relationship to others? How would I define my purpose?

Just like before, don't worry too much whether *you* would choose to live in this projected world. Focus on the kind of life that would unfold for a person if they chose to step across the threshold of this world and live according to its values and concerns.

Part 2: Interpret the Movie According to Your World

Interpret the film theologically. Having described it well, now discuss how this movie's vision of the world converges toward (is similar to) and diverges from (is different from) the world projected for us *by the gospel.* Then, ask yourself whether you would live in the world projected for you by this movie? Why or why not?

4

Settings of Theology: Behind the Page

That which was from the beginning, which we have heard, which we have seen with our eyes, which we have looked at and our hands have touched — this we proclaim concerning the Word of life.

— *1 John 1:1*

Architecture is communication from the body of the architect directly to the body of the person who encounters the work, perhaps centuries later.

— *Juhani Pallasmaa*[1]

Theology is composed by *persons.*

Maybe that seems too obvious, but I didn't appreciate it until my twenties when I traveled through Israel and Turkey studying the Jewish and Middle Eastern backgrounds of Christianity. I couldn't get enough of it! Jesus's Jewishness, his vocation as a rabbi, the kind of life you could expect as a disciple, ancient Middle Eastern habits of thought, the pagan religions of the cities to whom Paul wrote — all of it fascinated me, because it led me to a deeper understanding of the Bible's historical and cultural settings. This relates to what we have called the world *behind* the pages of Scripture.

There is also a world behind any work of theology, and engaging this world is a pathway for drawing close to a theological work. The worlds of the page and in front of it beckon as well. Yet, if we forgo the world of the author, her setting and her communities, then we depersonalize theology. Works of theology become dusty tomes and dead letters to us, rather than invitations.

In this chapter, we consider the world behind in terms of theology's settings, by which we mean the author as a person in her native environment. This includes the social and cultural dimensions of the author's setting and their theological texture. Every author is also involved in the providential movements of God, sometimes aware of her participation in God's movement in time and space but most often unaware of it. We will consider these dimensions one at a time: persons in *time*, in *communities*, and in *the providence of God*.

Persons

A work of theology is an author's vision of God and everything in light of God shared with readers through the medium of text. It is communication "fixed by writing."[2] A *person* stands behind whatever theology we read.

The too obvious fact of human authorship is often forgotten by students as they begin studying theology. The unfamiliar form and content of the readings consume their attention, and the author fades to the background. It is surprising how quickly this happens to the best of readers, especially considering that we exchange written communication throughout our days in texts and emails, never for an instant forgetting that a friend or family member composed them. Yet somehow theology falls into another category as we read it; words appear from nowhere and no one. How strange it would be to approach a sermon or testimony like this, but written theology often becomes a "thing" rather than a shared communication.

Could it be that we suppose the divine object of our study diminishes the importance of theology's human authors? Is human authorship less important because theology concerns God? One problem with this idea is the example of the New Testament. Given its God-inspired status, we might think that its human authorship does not matter. But looking at the New Testament, we find the contrary. The apostles accentuate rather than downplay their physical, embodied authorship to ground their *real* contact with the risen Christ. Their embodied personhood matters precisely because it is there – in time and space, in their bodies – that God meets them.

Consider John's witness to Jesus in 1 John. It turns entirely on John's *physical* encounter. The person of Christ whom John proclaims, the hope of the world, wasn't met through some out-of-body experience; instead, John goes out of his way to emphasize the real, tangible physicality of his relationship. John encountered Christ with all his senses.

> That which was from the beginning, which we have *heard*, which we have *seen* with our eyes, which we have *looked at* and our *hands have touched* – this we proclaim concerning the Word of life. The life appeared; we have *seen* it and testify to it. . . . We proclaim to you what we have *seen* and *heard*. (1 John 1:1, 2a, 3a, emphasis added)

We find no downplaying of John's embodied authorship here. He accentuates it. "I was really there," he stresses, "My eyes saw him and my ears heard him, and I touched him, and now that same person, I, *myself*, am writing to you." Christian readers have always heard in 1 John the words of God in and through this letter, but John ensures they can't overlook its human author.

When the human author disappears from our consciousness, we risk viewing theological works as inert objects rather than acts of communication cast forward to us by their author. When this happens, we lose our ability to engage them as invitations. Our posture toward them changes.

With this risk in mind, I bring the face of the author into the classroom whenever possible. For instance, when using PowerPoint to isolate important excerpts, I include a picture of the author. Seeing the author's face reminds us to contend with her words, to engage the space she created. More dramatically, and maybe comically, I bring a life-sized headshot to class. I tack it to a big piece of corkboard and prop it up, in a chair, at eye level. Because we sit in the round, the image of the author imaginatively brings her into the circle of conversation and dialogue. Its presence forms our imagination to receive the author's invitation to communicate, and thereby to get "closer" to her written work than we might if we thought of it as an inert object for us to do with as we please.

Before you chalk up the corkboard idea to the corny professor, let me add that it wasn't my idea (I wish it was!). A student once brought the board to class without warning and set it up in our circle. To Kody, our class discussions felt like real encounters with the author's communication, so it made sense to him that we should extend this into a tangible practice. I didn't argue. Thanks to Kody, the corkboard headshot continues to help us imagine reading as a living encounter with that author's world of meaning: the vision of a real person inviting real change.

Persons in Time

Saying an author is a person "in time" means his or her life unfolded across a range of specific years, days, and hours.

Imagine that you write a letter to your best friend in which you try your best to explain the significance of God. It's *your* letter, right? You signed your name at the bottom. The content came through you at the particular time you wrote, right? Ten years from now, if you wrote the letter again, would you write it the same way? Probably not. There would be similarities, of course. In both letters you might write about God's significance as Creator or as Redeemer, and you might also point back to the same moments at which all this became real to you. Yet so much else would be different. Everything about *you* ten years from now – who you are in that time – will inform what and how you write.

The same can be said of musical performance, as the world-renowned cellist Yo-Yo Ma describes it. The first piece of music he learned as a four-year-old was the Prelude to Bach's Cello Suite no. 1.

Now in his sixties, Ma has played it countless times, but each performance is slightly different because with each playing, *he* is slightly different: "I lived with this music for fifty-eight years . . . , so actually embedded in the way I play is actually *everything I've experienced*."[3]

Or consider Joseph, specifically the reunion with his brothers after all those years in Egypt (Gen. 50). Joseph's brothers sold him into slavery. In Egypt, he was mistreated and suffered many injustices, but he rose through the ranks of Egyptian politics, ultimately having a position of incredible influence. Because of his leadership, not only did Egypt have food stores during a famine but the surrounding nations flocked to Egypt for survival. Finally, after all this, he reunites with his brothers and says, "You intended to harm me, but God intended it for good to accomplish what is now being done, the saving of many lives" (Gen. 50:20).

Joseph's statement is incredible when you consider the time at which he said it. He didn't say it as a child, at home as his father's favorite son, or while languishing in a pit after his brothers faked his death and sold him off into slavery, or when he was wrongly accused and imprisoned, or when he won Pharaoh's favor. No. Joseph said, "God intended it for good" *after* the pit, and *after* the imprisonment, and only *after* he witnessed God working through him to bless the nations as they flocked to Egypt. It's Joseph's place in time that matters if we want to grasp the full significance of his words: "You intended to harm me, but God intended it for good."

Reflect on Chris's art for this chapter (the full image is on p. 74). Notice how he uses the hourglass to pull together the strands of Joseph's story. Joseph's time in the pit after his brothers' betrayal is part of the same life as their later embrace, so both appear in the hourglass together. Yet the significance of the embrace is only understood when we remember the pit. We have to hold them *together* to grasp the significance of the scene in which Joseph says, "You intended to harm me, but God intended it for good." An open hand rests below the hourglass, reaching up through the bottom of the frame and into the temporality of Joseph's life. As Joseph recognized, he was not the only author of his story. His destiny was being worked out by the hand of another. A theological imagination for reading trains us to expect no less for the authors of theology. Even when God's providence remains mysterious (as it most often does), we remain aware that the author's story is also written by the hand of another.

An author's place in time has three further dimensions: politics, ideas, and practices.[4]

Politics

As I'm using the word, "politics" names the church's relation to the unbelieving public, or "world" (or, as St. Augustine would say, "city"). Church and world are always related, and from one era to the next that relation changes, sometimes dramatically. The relationship between church and world, *politics*, continues to change.

The nature of the church-world relation colors the work of theology in that time. For instance, in the years following the death of the last apostle (the post-apostolic era), the Roman Empire frequently harassed the church. Because Christians refused to worship the gods of the Empire, the Romans thought them atheists. Others considered them cannibals for "eating" the body and blood of Christ at weekly Eucharistic celebrations. Some emperors violently persecuted them as threats to the peace of Rome. Thus, when reading theologians from the first centuries of the church, such as Ignatius of Antioch, Justin Martyr, or Tertullian, we shouldn't be surprised to discover that their theology is shot through with discussions of martyrdom and carefully reasoned arguments about Christian identity, designed to equip the faithful and to counter misconceptions.

Today, in the West, the political situation is different. Christians are not persecuted with the same ferocity or frequency as they were in early centuries (it's a different story in the Middle East). Our place in time thus presents a different relationship between church and world, and therefore different effects on our theology. For example, the twentieth century marked what many call the "death of God." This provocative phrase refers to a profound shift in how people think about the world and their place in it. Following the mass carnage of World War I, the idea of God, formerly taken for granted in Western society, seemed suddenly to have broken. "God is dead," wrote Hugo Ball in 1917. "A world has collapsed. . . . The world reveals itself to be a blind battle of forces unbound."[5] The Second World War only intensified the crisis of Western consciousness. This state of affairs has pushed some onto their heels and into defensive postures, while others embrace the opportunity to practice theology in a setting where nothing – *not even God* – can be taken for granted.

I could multiply examples, like anticolonialism, religious pluralism, gender politics, and the rise of religious extremism – all of which are factors today of the church-world relation in the West. My point is that theology's unavoidable situation *in time* always places it within the swirl of a particular church-world relation.

Ideas

In whatever time we live, we take some ideas for granted. For instance, before Copernicus (ca. 1520), people looked into the sky, watched the sun travel from one horizon to the other, and never doubted that *earth* was the center of creation. The sun and stars revolve around us, which generated a sense of primacy in the universe. And those who looked upon the heavens did not see the dark silence of space but a theater of sound, if they could only hear. As Robert Henryson put it,

> The heavens filled with stars so bright and clear,
> From East to West rolling their circles round;
> With every planet in its proper sphere,
> Sweetly emitting harmonies of sound.[6]

Read Dante's fourteenth-century masterpiece *The Divine Comedy* and you encounter an earth-centered cosmology wedded to theological convictions about God, heaven, hell, and purgatory. The earth's centrality in God's universe, and thus its cosmological centrality, was simply taken for granted.

Today, we take other ideas for granted. We imagine social spaces, like the voting booth or the debate stage, in which beliefs about God are removed. We call them "secular" spaces. As the idea goes in the West, religion has a place in society, but there should be other regions in which belief in God is absent. Until quite recently, no one considered such an idea![7] For Western people before the Enlightenment, *every* thing was held together by God at *every* moment of its existence. Nothing was thought to exist independently from God or disconnected from participation in God. It was simply taken for granted that all things, including society, participated in God. The idea of a secular space was not an idea anyone considered.[8]

Many ideas are in the air like that. We give them little thought. Like it or not, we must negotiate such ideas in theology, either running Christian thought "on their tracks" or resisting them. Our era's currency of thought sometimes serves theology well, opening up fresh perspectives. But other times it leads theology away from habits of thought that nourish and reinforce the practices of Christian faith. Sometimes, inhabiting theology from other eras and from other traditions can serve us well because their strangeness wakes us up to all that we've taken for granted or ignored.

Practices

A practice is a shared social activity. Like holding ideas unthinkingly, we often participate in practices without pausing to reflect on their meaning. For example, think of the last wedding or sporting event you attended, or the last mall you visited. Each drew you into a swirl of practices about which you probably didn't give a second thought (unless you were new to Western culture): standing when the bride appears, wearing team colors, gazing at and appraising products on display.

We don't think about most of our practices because they ride a wave of ideas and values that our communities take for granted. The unexamined practices of the mall, the sporting event, and the wedding pull us into the action and carry us along. The effect is not unlike liturgy (the sequence of practices in worship that every church has).[9] Like a church's liturgy, the liturgies of the mall and the sporting event form beliefs through our bodily participation in them. We come to believe *through* our bodies: gazing and purchasing, standing and sitting, cheering and booing, and so on. A church liturgy is crafted to awaken our need for God and form us to love our neighbors, while the mall's liturgy is just as carefully crafted to awaken feelings of need for more stuff. It forms us to love consumption.

Daily liturgies form us. This fact is no less true for authors of theology. Patristic Christians were formed by the practice of sharing with the poor the bread left over from the Eucharist. Byzantine Christians were formed by the practice of praying with icons and relics. Medieval Christians were formed by pilgrimage to holy sites. Reformation Christians were formed by martyrdom and the rediscovered practice of reading Scripture in their own language. Nineteenth-century evangelicals were formed by revivals. Contemporary Christians in the West are formed, whether we like it or not, by many nonreligious practices that form us just the same. We are persons *in time*, and our lives are full of practices we largely take for granted. These practices shape us.

Persons in Communities

Authors of theology are unavoidably enmeshed in communities. They have a family in which they are a son or daughter, and perhaps a brother or sister. In the course of life, they form various friendships and alliances, and they are mentored by people they admire. Sometimes the people they esteem in one season of life later become adversaries, and their theology becomes – painfully, I am sure – at odds with the heroes of earlier days. Marriage and parenthood may also be part of an author's life. The roles of husband or wife, father or mother, add to the storehouse of experiences and perspectives that inform their theology. Or, they may have lived during a time when theologians were predominantly celibate. Their deepest attachments were formed in the context of a stable monastic community. Such authors – Aelred of Rievaulx and Teresa of Ávila come to mind – may not personally know what it means to be spouses or parents, but they gave themselves fully to the gifts of friendship in Christian communities of service, study, and prayer.

All these communities are important, and attention to them helps us understand authors as embodied persons. My friend Laurie, a theology professor, believes this so strongly that she assigns the preface of course texts as required reading. Likewise, with all my assigned readings I include a paragraph called "ridiculously brief bio" in which I offer a few biographical remarks. Or consider my mother, who, for as long as I can remember, has refused to read a Christian writer before learning something about them. She gets it.

Another important community is an author's setting-of-origin (a clunky term, I know). This is the community within which an author primarily identifies herself as a theologian. Academy, church, workplace, or nonprofit organization: each of these will determine somewhat different terms for how theology is to be practiced. Sometimes an author's setting-of-origin matches her audience's, but not in every case. Consider an IRS agent. The setting of an IRS agent is the US government, which determines the terms for her work. Her audience, however, is the US taxpayer (who, in most cases, is not employed by the government). From her setting-of-origin in the government, and according to the expectations of that setting, the agent issues letters to plumbers, teachers, and wrestlers (who all hope they never get a letter from the IRS). In the same way, theologians also write *from* a setting-of-origin which determines the terms for their theology and *toward* an audience who may or may not share their setting.

Setting-of-origin is more important for the world behind theology than we might initially think. A brief history lesson will help (you might want to lean in; this will be intense).

Theology before the Nineteenth Century: One Setting, Two Audiences

From the early centuries of the church through roughly the eighteenth century, theology in large part had one setting-of-origin and two audiences. Writers of theology were located *within* the church: priests, bishops, presbyters, or leaders of monastic communities. Within the church, theology was practiced for the benefit of clergy and of laypeople (sermons, hymns, and letters). The second audience for theology was the world, the unbelieving public. One setting, two audiences.

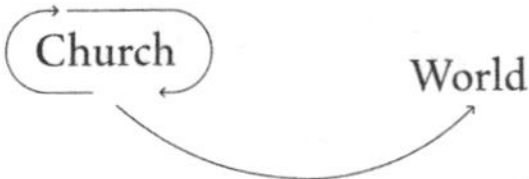

Laypeople have always been an audience for theology, especially prior to the nineteenth century. Bishops, priests, monastics, and the Reformers of the sixteenth century published sermons and sermon series to nurture faith. Hymns are theological works sung in church, like those written by Ephrem the Syrian in the fourth century or Charles Wesley in the eighteenth century. Through song they taught the faithful to believe rightly. Sixteenth-century Reformation-era Christians, Protestant *and* Catholic, used the recently invented printing press to distribute theological material to laypeople. And for illiterate Christians of every era, mosaics, icons, and paintings nurtured faith without words. In other cases, theology was composed for church leaders. Letters, sermons, disputations, and creeds served the church's worship, clarified belief, and galvanized mission.[10]

Universities emerged in the twelfth century, as centers of education shifted from rural monasteries to city cathedral schools.[11] We might imagine that the university was a new setting-of-origin for theology, distinct from the church, but we'd be wrong. Theology in the earliest European universities was still considered *church* theology in the sense that it was theology according to the beliefs, practices, and mission of the church (even as some pressed for reform, as we find with John Wycliff and William Tyndale). Theology in the early universities was "science," but, according to Thomas Aquinas, it was science in this sense: an *organized body of knowledge*.[12] Theology was commonly practiced as disputations or systems of doctrine, like Aquinas's *Summa Theologica*, but it was still considered discourse within the setting of the believing church and accountable to the church's tradition of faith.

Theology's second audience was the world. In early centuries, bishops and priests like Tertullian and Justin Martyr wrote letters to Roman officials to explain the Christian faith. In the medieval era, Islam increasingly encountered Christianity, often violently. Thus, theology was sometimes composed, as it was by theologian and philosopher Nicholas of Cusa in the fifteenth century, to clarify Christian beliefs in relation to the tenets of Islam. During the Reformation, Reformers – who included laypeople and women like Argula von Grumbach – sometimes argued their cause directly to city councils.

Theology after the Nineteenth Century: Two Settings, Three Audiences

Then, in the early years of the nineteenth century, theology gained a new setting-of-origin with expectations markedly different from the church. In 1810 the first "modern" university was founded: the University of Berlin.[13] It was a state-run institution in which theology – like all disciplines – served the German state and conformed to the expectations of modern science, now understood as neutral reason. Other sciences had no place for the authority of Scripture or the traditions of the church, so where did that leave theology? Theology in the university adapted. To many it seemed that "academic theology" had more in common with the world than with the church.

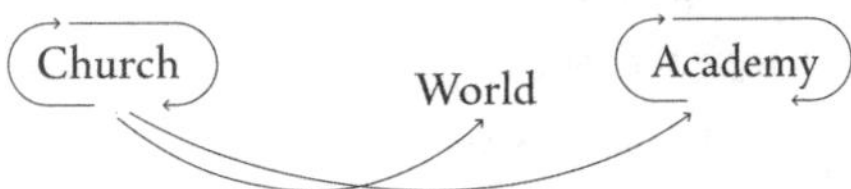

The modern scientific methods of the university brought dramatic changes to theology. The university and the church did not take for granted the same ideas, habits of thought, or practices.

> Western culture has come more and more to assume that the business of universities is not to reflect directly on religious faith or to promote religious practice. Religious thought and behavior, certainly, both individual and social, are understood to be worth studying in a scholarly way, as a highly influential aspect of human culture, a part of human history. But in a university, it is generally assumed, religion must be considered objectively, from the safe distance of the neutral observer; religious phenomena may be observed and measured, religious language analyzed, but the basic conviction of a worshipping community, living from and in a tradition of faith, needs to be kept separate from academic study, if the rules of scientific inquiry are to be rightly observed.[14]

The differences between church theology and university theology are sometimes breathtaking.

According to the standards of the modern university, for instance, the spiritual health of the theologian has no bearing on the practice of her "science," whereas in the church, one's nearness to God was essential to a theologian's work. St. Augustine of Hippo, for instance, argued that more important than a theologian's language skills and rhetorical power was her spiritual well-being.[15] Holiness preceded skill. As late as the fourteenth century, the Vienna theology faculty affirmed the necessity that the author of a work of theology be in fellowship with God and formed in virtue: "The spiritual eye must be very clear from sin in order to discern the lofty themes of theology. . . . The schools of theology must not be merely schools of science, but still more, schools of virtue and good morals."[16]

Where are we today? Two attitudes generally prevail about theology as it relates to university settings.

The first attitude champions the classic notion of theology. Sermons are delivered weekly for the believing community, songs and icons are created and shared, and some pastors even write theology *toward* the world. In seminaries and church-affiliated Christian universities, which are both extensions of the church (in most cases), theology is written for laypeople and ministers in the church, to the world, *and* to the academy. There is a spectrum of practice here, of course. On one end, theology is taken to be more "academic." Those who practice it more readily embrace the style, approaches, and habits of mind taken for granted in the secular academy. On the other end, authors of theology tend to be more critical of the academy's assumptions and norms.[17] On that side of the spectrum, theology might be less "academic" but isn't any less *rigorous*. The measures for "rigor" are set by other standards.[18]

The second attitude about theology celebrates the distance between church and academy. On this view, academic theology offers a necessary critical angle for theology – one not possible *within* the walls of the church. Academic theology at this end of the spectrum operates "at the intersection between two communities, . . . that of the church and that of the modern university."[19]

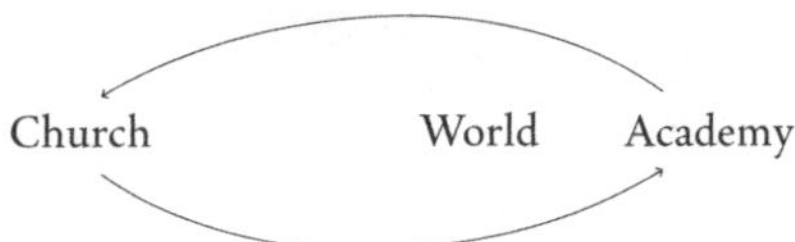

This approach to academic theology is critical and constructive. It seeks to reinterpret beliefs and practices through perspectives that are not native to the church. Theology performed in this setting doesn't assume beliefs and practices taken as given within the believing community but tests them and refracts them through other perspectives, ideas, habits of mind, and practices.

Persons in the Providence of God

Finally, we read theology against the backdrop of God's providence. "Providence" is the word we use in theology to name the exercise of God's lordship over the entire cosmos. Over and in everything and everyone, God is involved, invested, and Lord. Scripture teaches that God is the origin of all that is and remains *present* to creation, moving history forward according to his love, power, and wisdom. Creation and providence thus go together, as Paul shows: "The God who made the world and everything in it is the Lord of heaven and earth" (Acts 17:24). As *Lord*, God is no distant observer, nor is God a mere participant in history. God does not merely watch our comings and goings from far off, nor is God just another actor caught up in the drama. God is indeed an actor but not the same as created actors. The triune God of the gospel, the God of Abraham, Isaac, and Jacob, made known to us finally and truly through Jesus the Messiah, is the Living God, the Lord of heaven and earth.

So much turns on how we understand God as *Lord.* When we equate God's lordship with examples of human lordship, then we quickly stumble. We make terribly imperfect lords (because of sin), and our reach is so very limited (because of our finitude). As in all matters of theology, we must ensure that our theology of God's lordship is lordship proper *to God*. God's majestic particularity (he is God and no other), and therefore his particular majestic lordship rings out time and again in the Bible. In the second half of the verse quoted above, Paul makes precisely this move: contrary to what you might know of other lords, God "does not live in temples built by human hands. And he is not served by human hands, as if he needed anything. Rather, he himself gives everyone life and breath and everything else" (Acts 17:24–25; cf. Hosea 11:9 and Isa. 40–45). God is Lord according to his Godness, his unique being *as God*, which we know most tangibly in Jesus his Son.

We can say nothing more theologically basic about human life than this: we live within the sway of the unimaginably perfect and utterly sufficient lordship of God. As the psalmist said, "You go before me and follow me. You place your hand of blessing on my head" (Ps. 139:5 NLT). The same holds for the authors we read: our lives and theirs unfold within God's providential care and direction. "We are not simply agents . . . we are not just the authors of our biography. We are also those who are acted upon; we are also a text written by the hand of another."[20]

The providence of God is the theological backdrop for Jesus's teaching on anxiety. "Do not worry about your life"; instead, "Look at the birds of the air; they do not sow or reap or store away in barns, and yet your heavenly Father feeds them. Are you not much more valuable than they?" (Matt. 6:25–26). The smallest of birds are still objects of God's loving intentionality, his providential care. For James as well, God's providence is the theological scaffolding that supports his teaching on making plans while trusting God (James 4:13–17).

Simply put, God doesn't lose track of us, nor are his intentions for us ever vain, selfish, petty, or mean. Happily, no! According to his goodness, justice, and mercy, God is at work in and through all people, bringing the big and small to their ultimate fulfillment. This is what we mean when we talk about the providence of God.

Reading theology against a providential backdrop makes us *watchful.* We're on the lookout for the activity of God in the architecture of the author's work. I'm surely not claiming we can definitely and specifically know how God's at work. C. S. Lewis denies this possibility with his usual wit: "If, by one miracle, the total content of time were spread out before me, and if, by another, I were able to hold all that infinity of events in my mind, and if, by a third, God were pleased to comment on it so that I could understand it, then, to be sure, I could . . . read the meaning, discern the pattern. Yes; and if the sky fell we should all catch larks."[21] Lewis echoes the apostle Paul who (if anyone) we might suppose had special access to God's mind. Yet, after three chapters in Romans grappling with the election of Israel and the inclusion of the gentiles, he says, "Oh, the depth of the riches of the wisdom and knowledge of God! How unsearchable his judgments, and his paths beyond tracing out! 'Who has known the mind of the Lord? Or who has been his counselor?' . . . To him be the glory forever! Amen" (Rom. 11:33–34, 36).

It is not God's mind for which we're watchful when reading theology but God's "activity of sanctifying grace."[22] Such grace may appear through an author's work in the time and place in which it was written, or in times far afterward, even in the time of our own reading. Watchful reading is edge-of-our-seat reading as we look for God's holy-making activity ("sanctifying grace"). Again, it may be God's sanctifying grace in the author's life or in our own lives we see as we read. If we look for such work in our lives – watchful of the Spirit's activity, then seeking to join him in it – shouldn't we also be watchful for God's sanctifying work in and through the theology we read?

Second, we read *expectantly* that the Holy Spirit might conform us to the image of Christ through the theology of another. How the Spirit does so is certainly up to him: he may encourage us, challenge us, or even warn us. Remember, the authors we read were caught in the wake of new creation (like us), but this doesn't deny their missteps and errors (just as it doesn't deny ours). Some theology is rightly refuted and resisted, but the author we encounter remains – we hope – a brother or sister in Christ. We shouldn't be surprised if we praise an author one second and then pray for her in the next. Would we do any less with our friends?

Should We Read "Heretics"?

Some authors of theology believed what they wrote was true, though it was *false*. Should we read them?

The word "heresy" is used for a teaching that diverges from what Christians accept as correct, right, or "orthodox" (right – *orthos*; teaching – *doxa*). A Christian who holds onto that falsehood, and does so *stubbornly*, is a "heretic." She is not someone who merely believes incorrectly – none of us believes without error. Rather, a heretic is someone "who actively promotes" beliefs that she knows contradict widely accepted Christian teaching.[23] He or she "obstinately denies" a truth that Christians have collectively discerned as essential to the gospel while promoting some other teaching.[24]

"Heresy" and "heretic" are terms sometimes thrown around rather casually these days, but that hasn't been the historical norm. They are weighty words, not to be used hastily or glibly. In most cases, they were only applied after lengthy, communal deliberation, and only applied to core matters of faith.[25]

The collective wisdom of the Christian tradition treats heresy *seriously*. It's dangerous. It can warp our faith and thereby distort the shape of our presence in the world as followers of Christ. Considering the risks, should we read heretics from long ago, such as Arius (fourth century), who denied that Jesus shares the same divinity as the Father, or Pelagius (fourth century), who taught that we can be saved by our own efforts, or Apollinarius (fourth century), who denied that Jesus completely shares our humanity? And, though not considered "heresy" according to historical norms, should we read misguided authors from our recent past, such as James Henry Thornwell, who gave a theological rationale in *The Rights and Duties of Masters* (1850) for owning people as slaves? In terms of their potential to warp our faith, such beliefs are still dangerous, right?

In our day, the word "heresy" smacks of intolerance and exclusion, but it's essential in theology when used rightly. Not because it keeps sincerely misguided people on the outside, but rather because being Christian entails accepting particular truths by faith and rejecting particular falsehoods, even as we confess that our knowledge of truth is always partial. We hold onto the essential truths of our faith – such as the creation of the world by God, the divinity and humanity of Jesus the Messiah, and the gift of new life in Christ by God's grace – even as we acknowledge that our grasp on them is *never complete*. St. Anselm says it beautifully:

> No Christian ought to question the truth of what the Catholic Church believes in its heart and confesses with its mouth [by "Catholic" he means "universal"]. Rather, by holding constantly and unhesitatingly to this faith, by loving it and living according to it, he ought humbly, and as best as he is able, to seek to discover the reason why it is true. If he is able to understand, then let him give thanks to God. But if he cannot understand, then let him not toss his horns in strife but let him bow his head in reverence.[26]

We will never grasp the essential truths of our faith entirely (our theology is always ectypal), but in faith we accept them, hold onto them, seek to live by them, and pass them on – even as we revel in the depth that surpasses our understanding.

Thus, mindful of the risks, we should read heretics for at least the following two reasons. How we read them is also important, and I will return to that below.

First, we should read heretics to *avoid their mistakes*. None of us are above missteps and errors, and the moment we think otherwise, we're in trouble. In fact, supposing we are immune from repeating their mistakes is not merely prideful but itself false. Not one of us believes perfectly and not one of us is immune from sinning (an essential of Christian faith: we are not God), and to suppose otherwise is false. With this in mind, reading heretics can sharpen our ability to discern error both in ourselves and in our communities. They show us paths to avoid. In fact, some heresies persistently reappear in new forms among Christians throughout history, because some truths of our faith are difficult to travel rightly. For instance, holding onto the goodness of God's creation while avoiding the path of Gnosticism, or maintaining the authentic humanity of Jesus while avoiding the dead end of Apollinarius, who denied it. These dead ends reappear in new forms time and again.

Second, we should read heretics to *heighten our awareness* of our place in time, in communities, and in the providence of God. We may fall into error because we fail to appreciate how our context influences our theology. We take certain things for granted in our time and place, and such unthinking assumptions about the world, humanity, or culture can make heresy appear entirely reasonable. This has always been the case. Heretics believe something to be true that is in fact false, but such belief always has *context*. Understanding the context by engaging the world behind the text doesn't make it less false, but it helps us understand how it may have seemed true to the heretic. For example, the fourth-century bishop Apollinarius held a view of the human person that made it difficult for him to conceive how the humanity of God the Son extended to Jesus's human mind. Knowing this, my empathy for him significantly increases and my attentiveness to *my* context increases as well. What do I take for granted that could lead me to believe, teach, and live falsely?

These are reasons for reading heretics (despite the risks), but how should we read them?

First, we should read them *as an exercise in love*. I didn't say we should align ourselves with a heretic's vision of God, because truth matters. Theological truth matters most of all. Living according to God's revealed truth (along its grain) aligns us with God and his ways in the world – that's where we find abundant life, intellectually, emotionally, and volitionally. However, let's not forget that heretics are still persons in time, in communities, and in the providence of God. They are siblings in faith, and we should read them as such.[27] Moving "off the curb" and into an author's space does not require us to unpack our suitcases and settle in. We are not called to embrace an author's false vision . . . but we are called to love her, though you'd be hard-pressed to discern that by the way Christians often treat heretics. The heretic is still a person made in the image of God, and the demands of love are not diminished by her mistaken teaching.

Second, we should read them *as an exercise of empathy*. We engage them with the empathy that we'd hope others would offer us if we were in their place. St. Irenaeus of Lyons wrote a massive treatise in the second century against false teachers, called *Against Heresies*, and he didn't pull punches. He directly countered those whose teachings about Jesus diverged from the witness of the apostles, but he also *prayed* for them. He prayed that God would lead them to see and believe the truth: "Give to every reader of this book to know You, that You are God alone, and to be strengthened in You, and to shun every heretical, and godless, and impious doctrine."[28]

We do ourselves a great disservice – and I believe we sin – when we demonize heretics. They, like us, are frail and in need of Christ's consolation. By praying for them we open ourselves to the Holy Spirit in order to love like Jesus and see ourselves rightly: frail and needing the friendship of Jesus, just like heretics.

Third, we should read them *wisely*. At the end of chapter 7 I will have much more to say about the wisdom required for reading theology, but for now I'll offer this. The wise reader will engage heretics according to her maturity and her spiritual health. A new Christian should read orthodox sources, just like babies consume milk rather than steak (see Heb. 5 and 1 Cor. 3). Likewise, a Christian who is struggling in her faith, and thereby spiritually vulnerable, should avoid heresy. The wise reader should also engage heresy in community with mature believers and according to the "rules" (or guides) that keep us directed toward the truth even as we inhabit another person's theological space: the Rule of Scripture, the Rule of Faith, the Rule of Prayer, and the Rule of Love (flip ahead to chapter 7 for more on these).

All of this also applies to theologians who are not heretics but whose lives *fall short of our moral standards*. For instance, we find blistering anti-Semitism in latter writings of the sixteenth-century Reformer, Martin Luther. So you might wonder, "Why should I read some anti-Semite?!" Or, the twentieth-century theologian and civil rights leader Martin Luther King Jr. had extramarital affairs. Should we avoid him, too? This is not an easy matter. Not one of us can say our life seamlessly matches the truth we profess. Not you, dear reader, or me. Thus, I believe we should still read those who sin (like me) and love them by doing so. However, we should think carefully as we read about whether an author's moral failures reveal, in fact, something like a crack in the foundation of their theology that puts the whole structure at risk. This is not a light judgment, and we should only make it after much prayer.

Lord Jesus, help us.

Prayer

Providential God,
Somehow, you are Lord:
    other than us,
    but present with us,
        over,
        in,

and through all things.
Somehow, you are Lord:
active among us,
but your intentions for us are never
vain,
petty,
or mean,
but according to your
goodness,
justice,
and love.
Help us read theology watchful for your work in its author and expectant of your holy-making activity in us. Amen.

Summary

The world behind theology is the world of the author: a person in time, in communities, and in the providence of God. The world behind a work of theology is not the writing itself; rather, it is the person who composed it as they lived in a particular time, participated in particular social relations, and were drawn along by the providential movement of God in human history (so much of the latter remaining mysterious to us). Engaging the world behind a work helps the reader follow the arrows left by the author.

Questions for Reflection and Discussion

1. What are the "practices" from the rest of your life that most influence how you read theology? Are those practices helping or harming how you read?
2. Have you read theology expecting that God might use the activity to make you more like Jesus? If not, how could you change your expectations?

3. When has someone important to you written to communicate something meaningful to you? What needs to change in the way you read theology for it to feel that the same thing is happening as you read?

Theology Lab: Write a Letter

"How can this be?" Nicodemus asked.

—John 3:9

Sincere questions imply that I really want to hear the answer, and am not just looking for ways to display my own knowledge.

– David Smith[29]

This lab trains you to approach the author of the work you're reading as a person. Remember, the world behind a work of theology is the author's world. We learn about the author's world through studying their historical and cultural setting. Through understanding their setting, we are better able to follow the arrows they left us. We are better able to see the world they wish to project for us. But knowing all this, we can still treat theological texts like inert objects rather than dynamic spaces we are invited to enter and inhabit. Writing a letter personalizes the author. It makes them real *to you*.

Part 1

Address your recipient and introduce yourself (the "greeting"). Then identify and describe the feature of the author's teaching or witness that has made an impression on you (positive or negative). Describe it in such a way that it is clear that you fully comprehend what they believed and taught.

This part of the lab is about demonstrating comprehension of the content of the writings of the person with whom you chose to correspond by letter. Feel free to quote them if it does them the greatest honor, but work hard to put their arguments and positions in your own words. Show them that you have genuinely *heard* them!

Part 2

This part of the lab is about showing *theological hospitality*.

Can you *receive* your guest with *hospitality* and thus receive the *gifts* they offer? Having shown your recipient the honor of seeking to understand them, the second part of your letter should cross the bridge to your own situation. You could either *thank* them for their contribution to you or you could approach them with sincere, genuine questions. Any of the following questions would be appropriate to use as idea starters.

The author, like us, sought to contend for the gospel – *can you express to them how their theology benefits you today?*

The author, like us, struggled with the limitations of language to give expression to the mystery of Christ – *can you ask them questions for clarification, for them to explain something you would like to hear more about?*

The author, like us, did it all imperfectly – *even if you disagree with their theology, could you receive them as a legitimate conversation partner?*

The author, like us, was frail and in need of Christ's consolation – *can you reach out to them and speak to the needs you sense in them?*

Through letter writing, you reach across your differences in geography, culture, and time to engage your author as a human person. A neighbor made in the image of God.

Examples

In one of my classes, we inhabit writings on Christology from a handful of early church figures, then students compose a letter to one of them. They reach out to Irenaeus, Arius, Athanasius, Apollinarius, Gregory of Nazianzus, Gregory of Nyssa, or Cyril of Jerusalem. Here are a few samples.

I love this letter because the student asked Cyril a sincere clarifying question:

> Cyril of Alexandria, . . . the section about Jesus suffering brought a question to my mind. I was wondering if you could expound on your thought that the divine part of the Word of God does not suffer. Though I understand that Jesus, as you put it, suffered "blows or piercing with nails" because he had a human body, would he still not have suffered in other ways such as emotionally and mentally?

This student thanks Gregory by sharing how his Christology served her spiritual development:

> Gregory of Nazianzus, . . . Your writing has allowed me to dig deeper and that has allowed me to view myself in a new way. My abilities are far greater than I thought. I am a carefully crafted (though still imperfect) model of the perfected image of God, who is Christ Jesus. Each day I am being molded further into that perfected image. It's so awe-inspiring to think that the Father sent the Son to take on flesh to be the example of how to love, how to do outreach, how to operate in faith. He was *perfect*. Such a thing can only come from God. It is true divinity within humanity.

I admire this letter writer. While the student accurately sees the errors in Apollinarius's Christology, she still thanks him for trying to serve the church.

Dear Apollinarius, I appreciate so much your work in defending the divinity of Christ in the Arian controversy. Without your faith and hard work, my faith might be different today. There is a long chain of events that have happened since you walked the earth. However, the traditions of faith that you and others have passed down to me have helped me believe in Jesus Christ. While we would have been friends, we would have disagreed on some issues. This would not break our friendship, but would probably cause us to have many lively debates.

5

Sources of Theology: Of the Page

Beginning with Moses and all the Prophets, he interpreted to them what was said in all the Scriptures concerning himself.

— *Luke 24:27*

The architect is a sort of theatrical producer. . . . Innumerable circumstances are dependent on the way he arranges this setting for us. When his intentions succeed, he is like the perfect host who provides every comfort for his guests.

— *Steen Eiler Rasmussen*[1]

Can you imagine understanding a painting without ever looking at the canvas? Or an architectural space without being in it? You reserve your attention for its creator and the time and place in which it was made, but you never actually engage the work itself: the paints on the canvas and what it evokes in you, the ordered space of the building and how it affects you. It would be like trying to understand a work of theology without giving yourself to everything you find on the page.

In the world *of* theology, our attention rests on everything we find *on* the page. In this world we discover the arrows left for us and where they point. When we follow the arrows well (comprehension), aided by all that we learn from the world behind the page, then we encounter the world of meaning the author intends for us (understanding). We see as the author sees.

The world *of* theology is the space itself: its materials, how it's constructed, and the world it projects. In whatever kind of space we find ourselves in when reading theology – hospitable or hostile, inspiring or insipid – the materials are largely consistent. We call the materials "sources," and with them writers of theology construct the spaces we inhabit as readers.

Picture yourself walking into a building, turning to your neighbor, and the best you can say is, "Huh, concrete." You identified the material, but you couldn't discern *how* it's used. That's a problem. We know that physical spaces vary widely even as they are built from the same materials, right? Identical resources are used to construct a cathedral, a video arcade, or (at the risk of being dramatic) a gas chamber. What makes all the difference is *how* the materials are used and what they are used *for*. The same applies to theology. Recognizing the sources of theology is a big step forward, but still more important is recognizing *how* an author uses them.

What I'm going to recommend is this: we need an architect's eye for theology. Our eyes need to "roam about the room" of a theological text, noticing the materials of the space, discerning how they are used, and attending to their effect on us. What materials does the author use most prominently? What does their arrangement say about their importance to the author? And what does the space communicate about its subject? All such questions concern the sources of theology and their use: the world of the page.

The world *of* theology gets two chapters. This chapter considers theology's sources, and the next focuses on its architectures. In this chapter, we start developing an architect's eye for theology in three moves. First, we address the topic of God's revelation. Second, we consider the sources of theology. Third, we consider their relationship.

An Architect's Eye (Part 1): God Makes Himself Known

Our initial move may seem at first a rabbit trail, but there is little use addressing the sources of theology unless we accept a basic fact: theology is a *given* activity. What I mean is that our contemplation of God (theology) is always a response to God's self-revealing activity. As John Behr reminds us, "Theology begins and ends with the contemplation of the revelation of God, as he has shown himself to be. Anything else is not theology at all, but fantasy."[2] Theology does not spring unprompted from us.

We shouldn't pretend this feels natural. It runs against many of our embedded ways of thinking about initiative and action. We get up in the morning, set our course, and off we go. Something may hinder us, like another person or our physical limitations, but the act of getting up and going seems pretty well in our hands.

Christians, however, see things differently (or we should). First, we believe that God is the Creator of all that is, so to be at all is God's gift. *We are not self-creators.* Second, we believe God does not remain hidden but freely and graciously turns outward to us so we might know God and thereby fulfill our purpose as image-bearers: fellowship with God. *We are not self-initiators.* Third, we believe God graciously enlightens, or illumines, our perception from its darkness so that we perceive God's revelation. *We are not self-perceivers* (see 1 Cor. 2).

We like to think we jump-start theology, but it's not the case when the terms of theology are set by Christian teaching about creation, revelation, and illumination. God creates; God reveals; God illumines. I don't mean that our humanity and will are mere illusions. Rather, we do not discover God because of intuition, genius, or diligence, even as God *harnesses* such features of our embodied existence. God's revelation is "the making-known of what we truly *cannot* tell ourselves in and through the events we experience and in our language."[3] The means for revelation are many, but they are all God's. We come to God through his actions, like sustaining, judging, delivering, and so on. God also reveals himself through speech acts, such as covenant-making, declaring, promising, calling, and so on. And the most concrete revelation of Godself is the person of Jesus Christ who "radiates God's own glory and expresses the very character of God" (Heb. 1:3 NLT). Jesus simply *is* God's revelation.[4] These are God's invitations to seek and know him. God creates the possibility for theology.

This brings us to the channels and pathways to which we look as faith seeks to know God and everything in light of God. We commonly call these pathways "sources." As Thomas Oden explains, the sources of theology are

> those varied channels, means, or conveyances by which the divine address comes to humanity and an understanding of God is thus possible . . . [including] creation, providence, reason, conscience, beauty, and personal experience, as well as Scripture and tradition. Broadly speaking, the sources of theology include any means (whether natural, rational, moral, textual, liturgical, spiritual, or divinely revealed) by which the divine goodness is conveyed to humanity.[5]

The sources for theology are varied, but one feature is essential and constant: *God* acts through them. Revelation is *God's* revelation of *Godself* and its origin lies with *God*. The triune God comes to us that we may flourish, knowing him and ourselves truly. However much headway we make in theology, we are not the only agent authoring our progress.

This diagram correctly pictures divine revelation's origin, but it dreadfully misrepresents revelation in another, important way.

This next move may feel odd, but trust me.

Where is heaven? The question matters because heaven is the place from which God reveals himself to us. And if we think of heaven as up there in the clouds, then we're going to have a really hard time expecting much from theology's sources that are *down here* with us. Heaven isn't "up." Rather, it's the dimension where God rules and reigns, where God's will is done perfectly.

We easily misperceive heaven as up in the sky and above the clouds. In the Bible we find plenty of "up" references. The people of the Bible had a different cosmology than modern people. They imagined the physical cosmos and its relationship to God in terms of up and down. Good is up and bad is down. Not until Copernicus did new ways to perceive cosmology open up. The authors of the Bible spoke of God as "up" to express his exalted state, but the term "other" expresses the same idea better for us in our post-Copernican world. When we hear the word "heaven," Karl Barth helpfully explains,

> we are inclined to think of the great blue or grey sphere arching over us with its sunshine, its clouds and its rain, or of the even higher world of the stars. This is what we may have in mind right now. In the vocabulary of the Bible, however, this "heaven" is nothing but the sign of an even higher reality. . . . In biblical language heaven is the dwelling place, the throne, of God. It is the mystery *encompassing us everywhere. There* Jesus Christ lives. He is in the centre of this mystery beyond.[6]

The Living God is not up, down, or over there, because these are ways to talk about the spatial location of finite, physical beings. God is not a being like us – he is the Living God! Since God is not "up," neither is heaven "up."[7] Heaven is the mystery *encompassing us everywhere*.

Therefore, God is not up; God is *other*. The consequence of this for our perception of interacting with God is immediate and profound: God is nearer than we can think or imagine to any place or any person. In all the ways that finite, creaturely life limits us, God is *free*. For instance, since I am not God I knock against my daughter's elbows when I wrap her up in a hug. Our physical limits restrict our proximity to each other. Likewise, however hard I work to understand my own mind, I'm still a mystery to myself. The extent of my self-knowledge is limited, just like the extent of my arms' reach around my daughter. However (a *huge* however), God is free of our limitations.

God is *God*, the Living God, wholly and truly Godself, dependent on no one or nothing for life. God has life in himself (John 5:26).

God's *Godness*, therefore, doesn't make God distant, way up there in the clouds, but mind-bogglingly *near*.[8] God's radical otherness from creation (what we earlier discussed in terms of holiness and transcendence) enables God to be *nearer* to us than we can ever be to ourselves. God's transcendence doesn't mean that God is far away, but near in ways that are *only* fitting to God. This diagram is therefore better than the last at picturing divine revelation.

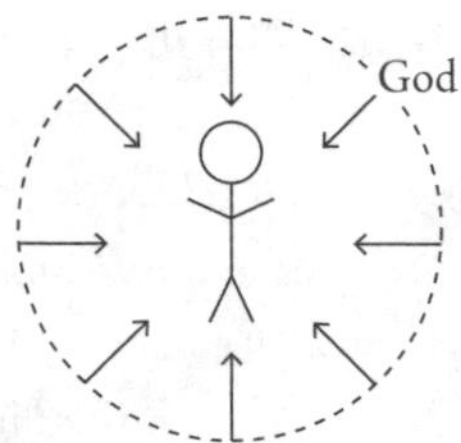

To understand how God uses the sources of theology, we must address them in terms of God's unique relation to the world. The last diagram did not represent this well. Notice in this diagram, however, how the arrows come from multiple angles. The origin of God's self-revealing activity is not limited to "up." God reveals himself *through* created things – the stuff around us and even the stuff in us. The origin of divine revelation remains God – always God – even as God meets us through physical and creaturely means.

If our diagram had just one bold arrow coming down, it would remind us that God is "above" us in the sense that he is great, awesome, and amazing. Yet, that picture which lurks in our minds has the unhappy consequence of limiting God's revelation to the mediating channels we most closely associate with divine things, like divinely authored Scripture or immediate experiences of the Holy Spirit. Imagining revelation as a big down arrow leads us to exclude both the physicality of theology's sources and our own physicality. We do not look to theology's sources because they are otherworldly but because they are means through which *God* is at work to make himself known.

Surely the most tangible illustration of God's taking up the material of creation to make himself known is the once-and-for-all incarnation of the Son in which God reveals himself *through human flesh*. The human body of Jesus is like the sources of theology in this way: both are inextricably part of the material world through which God reveals himself to us.

An Architect's Eye (Part 2): The Sources of Theology

All the varied channels through which faith seeks to know God and everything in light of God are traditionally separated into four categories – *Scripture, tradition, experience, reason* – and I'll suggest we add *culture.*[9] These are the materials of theology. Terms such as "norm," "warrant," and even "sources of authority" are sometimes used to describe them, because Christians look to these sources in order to ground and establish what they believe, teach, and profess.[10]

Holy Scripture: The Written Word

Holy Scripture is the collection of divinely inspired writings that we acknowledge as revelation *from* God and as a means *for* God's ongoing revelation. Scripture has its origin *with* God, "inspiration" (2 Tim. 3:16; 2 Pet. 1:21), and Scripture is brought to life in the heart of its reader *through* God, "illumination" (John 16:13–16; 1 Cor. 2:6–16; 3:5–7). In faith and ready expectation, Christians look to Holy Scripture to encounter God's living Word, Jesus the Son of God, who is "alive and active" (Heb. 4:12).[11] Scripture is often termed "special" revelation because it explicitly makes Jesus known, in contrast to "general" revelation in which transformative encounters with God happen outside of the church and without reference to Scripture, such as through creation, conscience, or culture. Throughout God's dealings with humanity, instances of special revelation include dreams, visions, angelic visitations, and direct encounters with God the Son or the Holy Spirit (think Ezekiel receiving the word of the Lord, Sarai and Abram with their three visitors, or Mary at the empty tomb). We also call Scripture "canonical," which means that this particular collection functions as a standard or measure for Christians. Holy Scripture universally includes the Old and New Testaments, and for some traditions, the Apocrypha.[12] Finally, among the sources of theology, Scripture and tradition function as "norms" or "warrants," meaning that we use them to interpret the other sources, and through them to ground and establish our knowledge of God. For Protestants (like myself), Holy Scripture is the *norm* by which all the others are understood, including tradition.

Tradition: The Word Remembered

Tradition refers, at its most basic, to the teaching of the apostles concerning Jesus the Messiah that is received and passed on by every generation. This is the sense of "tradition" that Paul uses when he says, "For what I received I passed on to you as of first importance" (1 Cor. 15:3; cf. Acts 2:42). We call tradition in this sense the "deposit of faith" (*depositum fidei*). More broadly, tradition refers to the core of Christian teaching – what is most essential to Christian witness – that we find in the early church creeds, such as the Nicene Creed (fourth century) and the Chalcedonian Creed (fifth century). Tradition in this sense is "The Great Tradition," for Christians have rallied around this creedal core for millennia, relying upon it like a basic grammar for faith and theology. Some Christians would also look to the church's most influential teachers and expect to find this same essential core, such as Irenaeus (second century), Augustine (fifth century), or Thomas Aquinas (thirteenth century). More broadly still, tradition can refer to individual traditions of worship, practice, and faith passed down within a particular branch of Christianity or even within a local congregation. Finally, most broadly, tradition can name the entire history of Christian witness: any person who confessed faith in Christ is part of the Christian tradition.

Experience: The Word Encountered

I see a good deal of confusion among Christians about the inclusion of *experience* as a source for theology. It's caused, I suspect, by the fact that we can mean a great many things by "experience." So, when it comes to theology, experience means just about everything or nothing. Let me, then, unpack experience a bit more than the last two sources, not because it's more important but because it's less understood. I'll first offer a tight description.

Experience is the perception of God given to us by the Holy Spirit, received by our senses through Scripture, through direct encounter with God (special revelation), or through creation, conscience, and culture (general revelation). This perception of God through our senses is a gift of grace and illumination whereby the Holy Spirit brings us into felt experience of the living Word, Jesus Christ. This is not experience in general but *revelatory experience*. Perceiving Jesus as the Messiah, the searing conviction of sin, the sense of God's nearness, or the awestruck silence of encountering God in creation are revelatory experiences. The Spirit may use such experiences for a myriad of purposes that are consistent with God's restorative work in the cosmos: to awaken our need for God prior to conversion, or to sustain, nurture, and develop faith in the process of sanctification.[13]

The meaning of experience, lest it drift into abstraction or take on whatever meaning we wish, must be grounded in Scripture and Christian tradition. Experience of this sort – revelatory experience – has four dimensions, and each permits experience to work as a source for theology in slightly different ways. First, we should mean the testimony of the Holy Spirit who confirms our adoption as children of God (Rom. 8:16; Gal. 4:6). This work of the Spirit is "ordinary," for it permeates every part of our lives as Christians and informs our theology at every turn. Second, we should mean extraordinary events within the flow of our days that stand apart from the common experience of everyday life. There have been a handful of times in my life when I knew I was standing on holy ground, that God was doing something that, when compared to the rest of my days, was astonishing and unique. Third, we should also mean the wisdom of following Jesus – the ordinary and extraordinary – which together forms a kind of "weight" or "resource" for theology. We might call it the *cumulative weight of discipleship* that gathers about people who live closely and consistently in fellowship with Jesus. I am referring to what accumulates as a result of a disciple's "long obedience in the same direction."[14] In the Christian tradition, we have called such people "saints," but most of us know such people. Like a seasoned craftsman who accumulates not only tools but also the artful knowledge for using them, saintly Christians can draw upon a life lived with God as a source for theology (maybe you or I will develop this capacity over many years).

Fourth, we should also mean the perception of God through our "spiritual senses." This term may be new to you, but it has a very long, diverse history among theologians – including early church figures like Origen of Alexandria and Gregory of Nyssa, eighteenth-century theologians such as John Wesley and Jonathan Edwards, as well as modern theologians like Hans Urs von Balthasar.[15] In short, spiritual senses enable us to perceive God in ways that are distinct from what our natural senses perceive, or as others would have it, are the result of the purification and refinement of our natural senses. Either way, we are talking about Spirit-enabled sensory capacities that are integral to Christian life and theology. "Faith," for instance, is "assurance about what we do not *see*" (Heb. 11:1), for it enables a kind of sight that is distinct from what our natural eyes offer. As John Wesley explains, our spiritual senses are "a new class of senses opened in your soul . . . to be the avenues to the invisible world, to discern spiritual objects. . . . And till you have these internal senses, till the eyes of your understanding are opened, you can have no apprehension of divine things, no idea of them at all."[16]

Something like this is in view when A. W. Tozer says, "A new set of eyes (so to speak) will develop within us enabling us to be looking at God while our outward eyes are seeing the scenes of this passing world."[17] Spiritual perception is part of our "journey of sanctification in which ever-new vistas open up," Sarah Coakley writes.[18]

How should experience be related to theology's other sources, like Scripture? That's a very good question, and I'll address it later in the chapter. I'll even picture and then explain my way of relating theology's sources – not so that you adopt my way, but to help you perceive and then refine yours.

Reason: The Word Made Intelligible

Reason refers to our rational reflection on and critical analysis of what we perceive, believe, assert, and do. Having perceived God through the many and diverse means through which the Holy Spirit makes God known to us, reason seeks understanding. Reason seeks not to master what God reveals, but to present Christian truth cohesively and intelligibly, avoid contradiction, and consider the historical and scientific knowledge available apart from Scripture (such as the physical sciences, philosophy, and mathematics).[19] Also, the use of reason itself – the *experience* of it – may be a means for revelation, for we use our minds as embodied persons; reasoning is part of bodily life. As we use intelligence – reflecting, questioning, parsing arguments, searching for coherence and harmony – God may reveal what would not have otherwise been perceived. We must be careful, however, to avoid casting reason as something autonomous, as if we use intelligence to wrestle something from God that was not his gift to those who seek him. Rational inquiry means "thinking *out of* revelation, yet in thinking it does not cease being active faith."[20]

Culture: The Hidden Word

Culture is the "meaning dimension" of social life.[21] It develops *in* and is projected *through* the works of meaning people produce: creative art, social customs, fashion, and forms of shared life and exchange like family, economy, and politics. These works of meaning express, transmit, and perpetuate a people's ideas, beliefs, and morality. As a source for theology, culture refers to the creative and expressive dimensions of shared human life through which we seek to discern the Holy Spirit's activity – even as that activity is often mysterious and hidden. Despite this quality of hiddenness, it is often worthwhile to attend to culture.

"In the creativity of God's finest creation – humankind – the Creator also speaks."[22]

We should pause again and spend a moment longer here, for not all theologians agree that culture is a legitimate source for theology.

My view is that, first, we should look to culture as the *context* for theology. It is a source in the sense that Christian perception, reflection, and embodiment always happen in particular times and places, and therefore within a particular *culture*. Thus, Christians should be mindful of culture in order to communicate the gospel intelligibly and winsomely. As Kutter Callaway explains,

> If theology and the Christian faith is going to be intelligible or make sense to anyone in the modern world, it really has to come from a place of being conversant with culture. We need to honor and respect the things we're engaged in dialogue with just as if it were a person sitting across a coffee table from us. One of the challenges for evangelical Christians is that we're not very good at being conversationalists. We tend to speak before we listen, and when we do that, we're not actually hearing what the culture is saying.[23]

The apostle Paul mirrors this use of culture in Acts 17. Walking through Athens, Paul notes how the Athenians worship, then he brings his awareness of their culture to bear when presenting Christ. In this sense, culture also opens fresh and unexpected avenues for understanding truth, goodness, and beauty.[24] This was also St. Augustine's approach when he advised that Christians "plunder the Egyptians." He meant we should use the best from non-Christian thinkers in order to comprehend and express the good news of Jesus.

Like it or not, we and our theology are embedded in culture(s), as the diagram on page 114 portrays. Evangelists translate the Bible into other people's native languages, theologians explore fresh angles on the gospel through cultural references, and pastors preach in languages other than Greek, because few in their church culture would understand it. Preachers "translate doctrine" so Christians can understand it and put it into practice.[25] (I am mindful of this even now as I write.)

Second, we should look to culture to discover the *hidden Word.* It is worth recalling how Scripture and tradition operate as norms, since we should approach culture differently. Culture is a field of general revelation, and thus a different kind of source from Scripture or tradition, which explicitly point us to Jesus, and thereby to specific, particular knowledge of the triune God of the gospel (i.e., special revelation). We should approach culture differently, more as we approach revelatory, transformative experiences that happen to us outside the church and without reference to Scripture or Jesus Christ. The revelatory experiences the Spirit awakens in us through cultural works of meaning like film and literature are more like the experiences had through conscience or in creation than like those had through Scripture or tradition. This way of describing the Spirit's revelatory activity through the works of culture, what I'm calling the *hidden Word,* is often called by others common grace, prevenient grace, or natural revelation.[26]

We look to works of culture to discern the hidden, mysterious, and prevenient activity of the Spirit, who reveals the Son. This even means that we seek to find God present and active in works that aren't *knowingly* directed toward God or produced by those who acknowledge him. Think of Paul again. Why did he cite pagan literature in his speech to the philosophers at the Areopagus (Acts 17)? Would Paul have said something untrue just to connect with his audience? He knew it would connect, but he also believed that in those particular words truth *resided.* They represented the way things are *truthfully*. They told the true story, even if not the whole story.

All truth is God's truth, the old saying goes, and the deep theological center of that statement is something like this: in all truth, in whatever resonates with how things really are, wherever it's found, the Spirit of truth is present and active, even among those who don't acknowledge him. John Calvin said that all people have a sense of God: "There is within the human mind, and indeed by natural instinct, an awareness of divinity."[27] If this is so, shouldn't we earnestly expect the Holy Spirit to be unexpectedly active in people who have a sense for him, and therefore discernibly present in the cultural works they produce? Said another way, because we cannot be certain in whom the Spirit is active or how he is working, shouldn't we hope that he is drawing people to himself, revealing the truth of Christ, leading them to conversion (as Jesus said he would be) – and therefore surprisingly present in the works of culture those people produce?

This the case for us, right? Before our conversion, the Spirit was present and active, graciously leading us to God. Therefore, shouldn't we be attentive for the same activity in others and thus attentive for where in culture we might find the hidden Word?

To summarize: the sources of theology are responses and channels. They are *responses* to God's self-revealing activity, even in cases of cultural works, when one may not realize they are responding to revelation. The sources of theology are also *channels*. To God's activity each source uniquely responds, and through each source God is graciously and transformatively present and active, enlivening, convicting, and strengthening.

The Road to Emmaus and the Meal

In order to understand the role of sources in theology better, consider Jesus's walk with his disciples on the road to Emmaus. It illustrates how Scripture can be a source of past revelation and a channel for ongoing revelation (Luke 24).

Jesus meets his disciples as they walk from Jerusalem to Emmaus. They were present for Jesus's crucifixion, but despite hearing rumors of his resurrection, they were utterly without hope. Their Messiah was dead. Their hope for the kingdom of God was dashed. Then Jesus ap-

pears, walking beside them, but they are prevented from recognizing him. Rowan Williams's poem "Emmaus" perfectly evokes their disorientation:

First the sun, then the shadow,
so that I screw my eyes to see
my friend's face, and its lines seem
different, and the voice shakes in the hot air

. . . .

When our eyes meet, I see bewilderment
(like mine); we cannot learn
this rhythm we are asked to walk,
and what we hear is not each other.[28]

Jesus's friends are bewildered by the experience of being with him. He is not only a stranger to them but he makes them strangers to each other: "I screw my eyes to see my friend's face, and its lines seem different." They don't recognize him, but he's reworking them, reforming them, shaking their settled sense of self, even their perception of the other.

The conversation turns to the events in Jerusalem. They are stunned Jesus hasn't heard (at least he doesn't let on), and they catch him up. Israel's hope, Jesus, is crucified. That morning some women found his grave empty and saw angels who said he was alive, but they didn't know what to make of all that. They were women after all, and among Jesus's peers that meant their testimony was worth nothing.

Jesus is frustrated: "How foolish you are, and how slow to believe all that the prophets have spoken" (Luke 24:25). They had the words of the prophets in Scripture. God *had spoken* to the prophets, and the disciples had their words as means of revelation.

Possession of texts wasn't their problem. Their faulty interpretation hindered them, so Jesus uses the Scriptures as means of God's *ongoing revelation*: "And beginning with Moses and all the Prophets, he explained to them what was said in all the Scriptures concerning himself" (Luke 24:27).

Why didn't Jesus pull back heaven's curtain to unmistakably reveal himself? Why not make himself known through another Mt. Tabor transfiguration or the Father's voice as it was heard at his baptism? Rather than using theophany (a term used to describe a manifestation or vision of God), Jesus chose the textual space of Scripture. He took the words of Moses and the prophets recorded in Scripture – responses to God's revelation to Moses and the prophets – and he used them as channels of God's revelation. He used Scripture to show himself.

However, the story doesn't end with Bible study. The text gives no indication that the disciples perceived Jesus through his teaching of Scripture. As it turned out, they finally perceived Jesus's face through objects more mundane, objects more readily perceived as the "stuff" of creation. At dinner, Jesus took bread in his hands. When he broke it, which was an entirely normal action, "their eyes were opened and they recognized him" (Luke 24:31). Breaking ordinary bread, at an ordinary table, during an ordinary meal was a means of revelation in the hands of Jesus.

Think about that. Jesus used Scripture *and* table practices. What can we learn from Christ's interaction with these disciples? First, we should remain vigilantly attentive for God's revelatory presence in the places where we are accustomed to look, namely the objective sources of Scripture and tradition. Second, I believe we should increase our attentiveness for God's revelatory presence in the seemingly *ordinary*, material stuff of everyday life. Outside Scripture and tradition, we may encounter the intimacy of God's revelatory presence in the experience of Christ when celebrating the sacraments, or be overcome by awestruck wonder in creation, or experience the fellowship of the Trinity through spiritual friends, directors, and family. As Ellen Charry writes, "The hope [of Christian experience] is to internalize and personalize the doctrines, practices, decrees, and ordinances of the church. . . . [Christian experience] is spontaneous, emotional, unpredictable, perhaps even disconcerting, and, in its more evangelical forms, associated with the most dynamic and spontaneous person of the Trinity, the Holy Spirit."[29] The Holy Spirit works to reach some through the written Word, some through the preached Word, some through observing those whose lives are shaped by that Word, and some through what seem to be direct encounters with the Living Word. Praise God for them all! God can even use a theology book to reach you (even if you initially had low expectations for it).

An Architect's Eye (Part 3): The Sources Related

If we look for God's revelatory presence in all of theology's sources, then how should we relate them? In other words, as we seek to know God and everything in light of God, is there Christian wisdom for how the materials of theology are *put together*?

This is an important, long-standing question, and not everyone answers it in the same way. Christians have recognized that while all the sources are responses and channels of God's revelation, they differ in kind. They are not identical cogs in a machine, nor the same sort of building materials. Christians have also recognized (the great majority of us across history, anyway) that Scripture and tradition are materials with a *foundational* role. Said differently, they have interpretive *priority* in relation to the other sources. This means, for example, that we look to Scripture in the light of tradition to interpret experiences of God's revelatory presence without depleting the importance of those experiences. Our knowledge of God's character and will are *grounded* in and *established* by our reading of Scripture in the light of tradition.

This does not mean we interpret Scripture outside our personal experiences. Let's not kid ourselves. Interpretation is always already a bodily act. Rather, it means that we should read Scripture in the company of other Christians, present and past. We ought to read Scripture together to cover our blind spots and open up fresh perspectives. We read Scripture in community so as not to forget what remains most central: Christ, God's promised Messiah, the hope of the world.

The example of Emmaus and the meal is again suggestive. Jesus brought his disciples to Scripture *first*. The Scripture as source, the written Word, has interpretive priority for us, even though Scripture is subjectively interpreted (by human interpreters). Following the pattern of Jesus, therefore, the vast majority of Christian theologians seek to employ *every* source while looking expectantly to Scripture as the "central preconditioning source."[30] Think of Scripture like a keystone that establishes an archway, or the cornerstone of a wall, or the foundation of a building, or – a metaphor I prefer – the *center of gravity* that draws the other sources into its orbit, setting their course.

How Do You *Map the Sources?*

I have my theology students represent how they understand the relationship between sources by visually mapping them with some kind of image. It's an incredibly useful exercise (see Theology Lab 5). Some students use static images, like a building with Scripture as its foundation or a painting with tradition as the frame. Others use images that present the sources in dynamic, cyclical movement, one source moving to another and to another, and so on; I've seen examples that use rivers, pathways, organic systems, or the cooperating aspects of a tricycle. I'm continually surprised year after year!

The exercise reveals each student's *embedded theology*. Their preconceived and often unexamined ideas, beliefs, and conceptions are revealed in the image. They complete the exercise outside of class, then we reconvene and students draw their images on the board and present them to everyone. After we observe and listen, we get to ask charitable, direct questions: Why did you choose that image? What do you mean for it to communicate? Why do you believe that? I ask my own questions as well, and I point out the patterns I'm noticing across everyone's pictures.

What is happening as we map the sources? First, students are gaining an architect's eye for their own theological spaces, ones that are not published between two covers but exist in them. Second, it increases their ability to apply that eye to the works of theology we read together. If they can spot the materials of theology in their own beliefs *and* articulate how they relate, then they are primed for the same with their readings. Third, and equally important to me, their empathy increases dramatically for students who map the sources differently.

To help you imagine the activity, I want you to see how I map the sources. I also want to help you glimpse the world behind the pages of this book – *my* world as the author. My diagram is certainly not the only way to visualize this relationship, nor is it final for me. I'm still learning and growing. My sense for these relations may change, or my students might teach me a better way to depict it. Take a close look at the diagram. What do you notice? What would you like to ask me? How does it differ from your instincts? How is it similar?

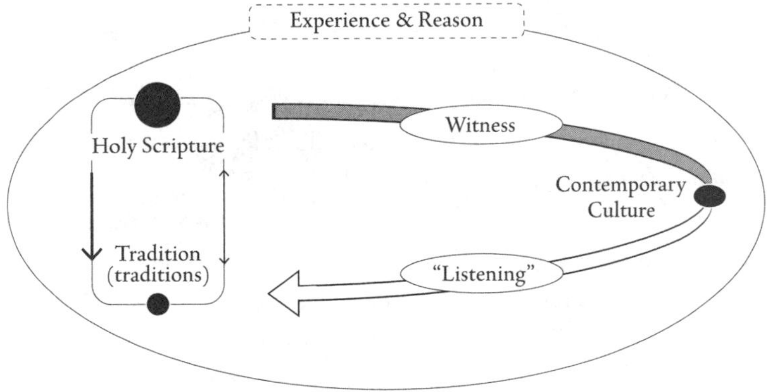

I'd like for you to notice three things (a common way for my students to begin as they explain their scrawlings on the chalkboard).

First, note the oval surrounding everything. I believe we practice theology, inescapably, within our experience of faith and within our intellectual capacity. Thus, the oval represents our embodied life in terms of experience and reason. It pictures that we practice theology within the frame of our particular life – not just any experiences and reason, but *our* application of them. We cannot avoid this, nor do I believe we should seek to avoid this. Second, notice the arrows going up and down between Scripture and tradition. I understand their relation as a feedback loop. The arrow from Scripture toward tradition is thicker, for I believe Scripture tests, disciplines, and establishes tradition. Tradition helps us interpret Scripture, but Scripture grounds tradition. Third, note how contemporary culture has an arrow going to it and away from it. Culture is a source for theology in the following two senses: works of culture – like poetry, fiction, visual art, music, film, and so on – are *resources* for contextualizing the gospel and *channels* for the Spirit's surprising, prevenient activity. To depict the former, the arrow moves through "witness" away from Scripture and tradition *toward* culture. To show the latter, the arrow extends away from culture and back toward Scripture and tradition, this one called "listening." If you have a low view of culture, that may seem surprising, but I believe we may find the Spirit's *revelatory presence* surprisingly at work *through* works of culture.

Now let me take you even *further* behind the page by letting you in on a couple things about me that you couldn't learn from studying my drawing (no matter how hard you looked).

First, my sense of self as an Anglican Christian also shapes the feedback loop between Scripture and tradition. On one hand, the down arrow is bold because, as a Protestant follower of Christ, I value the Reformation principle, "always being reformed according to the Word of God" (*ecclesia reformata, semper reformanda secundum verbum Dei*). Thus, I seek to stand responsible and pliable before Holy Scripture so that the Holy Spirit can reform and renovate every aspect of me (Heb. 12; John 14, 16). I receive the Christian tradition joyfully but critically and always along the grain of Scripture (as when you make wood smooth by sanding along the grain). On the other hand, the up arrow is bold and clear because I believe the church is one and universal, as the Nicene Creed says it. This nurtures a way of interacting with the Christian past called "retrieval." I do not believe we find strangers when we look backward in time. We find siblings in Christ who are united to us through our shared inclusion in the body of Christ. As I read Scripture and seek to follow Jesus, I consciously look backward for wisdom and insights.[31]

Second, the incarnation of God the Son matters deeply to me. It matters, of course, because Jesus inaugurates the kingdom of God on earth, but it also matters for my practice of theology. We believe that God drew near to creation to restore and heal creation; Christ took our flesh authentically and truly and entirely in order to heal our flesh – all of it, every bit, nothing left out. I believe this means something for theology. It means I value bodily experiences of God's revelatory presence and want to remain attentive in my theology to all the ways that my embodied life can be an avenue for seeking to know God and everything in light of God. That oval around the entire diagram, which represents experience and reason, is real for me. The way I value the incarnation also validates works of culture as sources for theology, especially when joined with a strong sense of the Holy Spirit's activity in creation and in our lives.

Dear reader, not everyone sees theology as I do. Others map the sources differently and have their reasons. I don't offer mine to convince you but only to help develop your architect's eye. And, to be entirely honest, I want to help you roam further into *this* space. As every author does, I want you to *inhabit* the space I've created for you. If I can help you encounter my world of meaning, then hopefully you will do so again and again with all those you read after closing these covers.

Why would I hope for less?

Prayer

Revealing God,
You took the strange shape of
enfleshment,
and you made your way among us:
skin,
fingernails,
and parched lips;
family,
friendships,
and betrayals;
truly,
really,
made like us in all respects except sinfulness.
Help us read theology poised for the activity to be, like tangible bread and wine in your hands, a means of showing us Jesus. Amen.

Summary

The world of theology includes the sources of theology. Each source is a response to God's revelation and a channel of God's ongoing revelation. The sources of theology are Scripture, tradition, reason, experience, and culture. From these materials, the architectural communication space of theology is constructed. Inhabiting theology requires an architect's eye, the most basic element of which is the identification of theology's sources as we see them being used.

Questions for Reflection and Discussion

1. Why is it significant that God is the one who reveals God, that we are not the ultimate initiators of theology?

2. In your faith journey, what sources or "channels" of God's revelation have been most emphasized?
3. How are the sources of theology related to each other in your life?

Theology Lab: Diagram Your Sources

> *Beginning with Moses and all the Prophets, he interpreted to them what was said in all the Scriptures concerning himself.*
>
> *– Luke 24:27*

> *By what authority or on what ground does Christian teaching rest? How does the worshipping community know what it seems to know?*
>
> *– Thomas Oden*[32]

Through this lab you discover how you relate the sources of theology to each other. It is an exercise that sharpens your architect's eye. It works like this: if you understand how you relate the sources of theology – if you can picture that relationship in your mind – then your eye for spotting the relationship between sources in theological readings is far greater. Said differently, you have to know the architecture of your own theology if you expect to discern the architecture of your author's theology.

Please do not pressure yourself to create a once-and-for-all diagram here. This is not about final decisions; rather, it's an active experiment in discerning what you already believe, your embedded theology. Embedded theology is a real thing for everyone, but few are aware of it. This lab provides structure for reflecting on and visually representing your already-on-board beliefs about the sources of theology. Trust me; you probably already know more than you think.

Part 1: Define the Sources

Refer to the definitions in chapter 3, and then, using your own words, define the sources of theology in no more than two sentences each.

Scripture
Tradition
Experience
Reason
Culture

Part 2: Describe How the Sources Relate

Describe and justify how you understand the relationship between theology's sources. This is your embedded theology of the sources. Is it a hierarchy for you (one source is most important, another second, another third, etc.)? Why? Do you see them arranged in a cycle (one source leads to the next, and to the next, etc.)? Why? Maybe you see their relationship another way. Try to explain your understanding and give reasons for why you see it this way. How do the sources of theology relate?

Part 3: Draw It and Share It

On a full sheet of paper, draw the relationship you just described. Don't be insecure about your artistic abilities, because artistic excellence is not the point. Visualizing the relationship between the sources and then drawing it will help you understand what you put into words. Seeing it, you will better understand it.

This lab is best completed with friends. Gather other theology readers and complete the lab separately, then get together to share your drawings. The experience seems to work best when you draw it and explain it to each other at the same time. Ask each other questions: "Why did you put that there? What does that image mean for you?" You will inevitably notice that your friends explained and drew the sources differently than you. Ask them questions that reflect receptivity (they may have something to teach you), hospitality (you have sincere questions for them), and empathy (you are trying to see as they see).

6

Architectures of Theology: Of the Page

Oh, the depth of the riches of the wisdom and knowledge of God! How unsearchable his judgments, and his paths beyond tracing out!

— *Romans 11:33*

Every building or space has its characteristic sound of intimacy or monumentality, invitation or rejection, hospitality or hostility.

— *Juhani Pallasmaa*[1]

We stay with the world *of* theology for another chapter, but in this chapter our attention shifts from theology's sources to its *architectures.*

As with any building, a work of theology has architecture. It has shape and form. It has materials, of course; those are the sources of theology. But the materials are built into an architectural space that communicates a world of meaning. As readers, we need an architect's eye so we can say more than, "Huh, concrete." Noticing such details is a good start, but there's more to understanding what a given space has to say. That *more* is communicated through its architecture.

This chapter has three parts and a question. First, I introduce the most common *approaches* to theology. Second, we consider some of theology's *forms.* Third, we examine three distinct *modes* of theology: worship, witness, and critique. Fourth, we address a question that arises in thinking about critique: what happens when theology "fails"?

Approaches to Theology

Theology became a university discipline in the nineteenth century, with an unexpected and far-reaching effect: the academic arrangement of the sciences splintered the once-unified practice of theology.[2] The following explanation runs the risk of oversimplifying a complex situation, but essentially the modern university had to figure out what to do with theologians, so it moved the textual dimension of their work to the ancient literature department, the historical dimension of their work to the history department, the metaphysical dimension of their work to the philosophy department, and so on. Five approaches to theology have been common ever since. Each approach has generated communities of writers, academic guilds, publishing houses, and journals dedicated to developing and furthering it. These five are especially recognizable in the curriculum and office layouts of most universities and seminaries.

The following definitions have limitations, of course. Each approach deserves greater nuance, but I would need many more pages for that. Thus, mindful of their limitations, I offer definitions that paint the landscape of theology with a broad brush. I frame each approach in terms of what it *looks at* and what it *aims to do*.

Biblical Theology

Biblical theology covers a remarkably wide array of approaches centered on Holy Scripture itself.[3] Biblical theologians often look at the whole of Scripture, searching for patterns and themes stretching across its entire scope. Themes like covenant, blessing, or the kingdom of God are regarded as windows into Scripture's unity and direction.

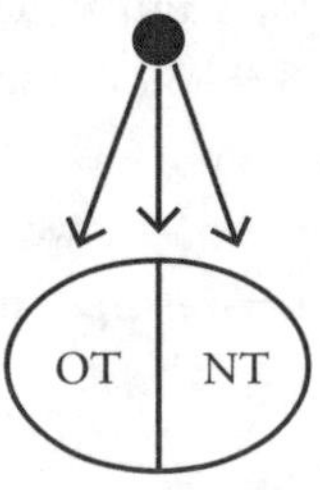

Other biblical theologians study the relationship between the two Testaments, consider issues of interpretation (hermeneutics), explore the cultural and historical backgrounds of the Bible, or study distinct theologies within Scripture (like the theology of Isaiah, Paul, or Jeremiah). In its most general sense, the term "biblical theology" is an approach that attends to the canon of Holy Scripture – its grand, overarching narrative, structure, and content.

Historical Theology

Historical theology is an approach that looks at particular historical settings to understand what Christians believe, profess, and do in that particular time and place and how Christian beliefs and practices may have changed over time. Theologians employing this approach may focus on official church teachings, on individuals, or on communities of faith that fall along the margins of the church. Rather than determine what the church should say now, though that may be a secondary aim, the primary aim of historical theology is to clarify and expound what the church did in fact believe, say, or do in the past.[4]

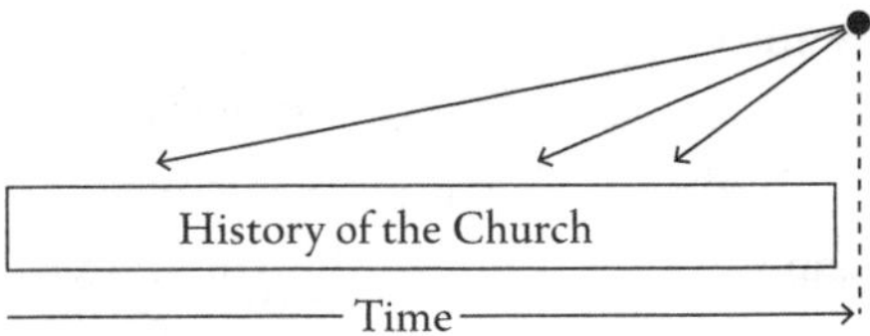

A work of historical theology might focus on the Nicene theology of the fourth century, fourth-century bishop Hilary of Poitiers's doctrine of the Trinity, or Protestant theology in the nineteenth century.[5]

Systematic Theology

Systematic theology is an approach that draws upon and integrates the previous two with the contemporary church and world in mind. Systematic theologians typically look at the content of Christian teaching (doctrine) as a unified, coherent, and interrelated whole. They explore this body of teaching and apply it constructively in response to opportunities, issues, or questions facing the contemporary church. Sometimes called "dogmatics" or "constructive" theology, this approach is not always systematic in the sense that it builds elaborate systems, but systematic as an approach to the whole of Christian teaching that is orderly, methodical, comprehensive, and integrative.

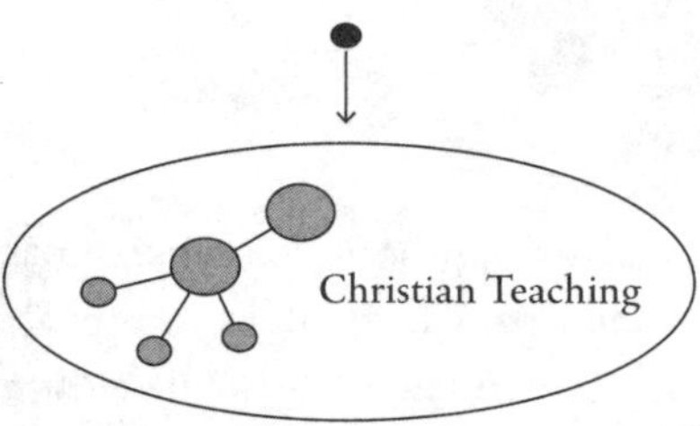

As Geerhardus Vos helpfully describes systematic theology, this approach draws a "circle" around Christian doctrine to explore the dynamics of the whole, for the sake of the contemporary church.[6]

Practical Theology

Practical theology first developed as a distinct approach in the nineteenth century to train ministers in the "practical" matters of church ministry (weddings, funerals, etc.). Today the approach focuses less on the duties of ministers and more on interpreting what the church *does* as it participates in God's mission: it is "critical reflection on the actions of the church in light of the gospel and Christian tradition."[7] It looks through the lens of Christian teaching at the church's life within the mission of God.

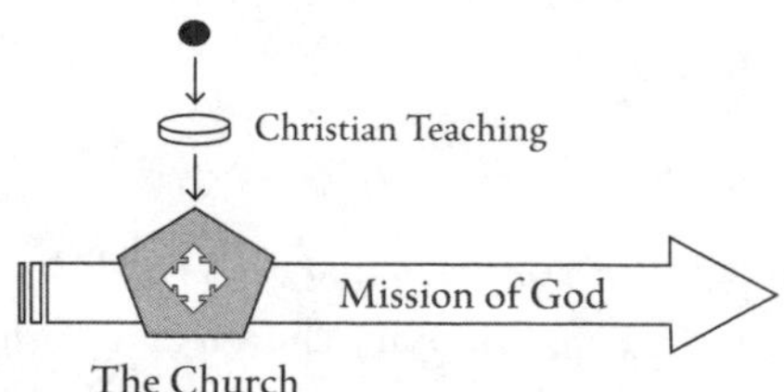

Practical theology focuses on Christian actions in the church's worship, discipleship, and social ethics (called "praxis") to consider how these reveal or conceal Christian teaching and how well they align with God's mission to redeem, restore, and reconcile.[8]

Philosophical Theology

Philosophical theology looks at Christian belief through philosophical tools and methods. Its purposes are many and varied. In some instances, it centers on analyzing "the concepts theology makes use of," like God, the soul, causation, time, and knowledge.[9] In other cases, it addresses traditional metaphysical questions from a distinctly Christian perspective or studies Christian teaching using the tools and methods of philosophy prevalent at the time.

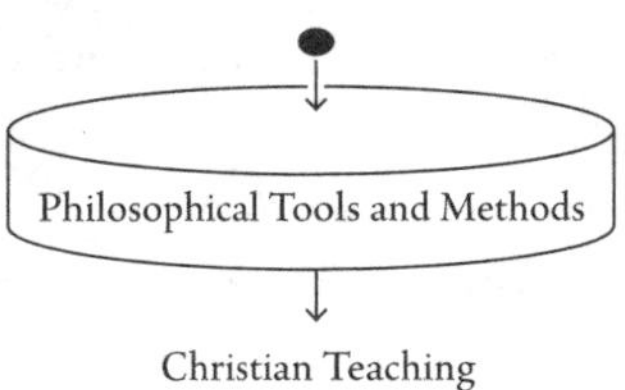

We have now considered five approaches that have schools, journals, and academic meetings dedicated to them. Let me mention two more.

Blended Approaches to Theology

Blended approaches are found in many works, past and present, and especially in those composed for nonspecialist readers. In this way of working, a theologian picks up one and then another approach, using them as needed to construct her space. The lines between approaches may sometimes blur as each contributes to the overall structure. Each approach offers its own perspective, like a window.

Imagine yourself in a room with windows, each offering a different view, as in Raoul Dufy's painting *Interior with Open Windows* (see p. 196). From one window, the arc of the coastline of the Riviera dominates your view, but you can only glimpse the edge of the city of Nice. The city dominates your view from the other window, climbing up from the beach, into the hills, and toward the sky. What could you see if more windows were present on your right and left? We can only imagine. Perhaps they would show fruit trees in the garden below, or the ocean stretching to the horizon.

You get the idea: each window, like each approach to theology, offers a unique view of the whole from which some features are entirely clear but others are hard to see or hidden altogether. We need the perspective from each to get the most comprehensive view. Before the modern era splintered the practice, theology was more easily integrated because theologians were primarily pastors and spiritual guides.[10] They integrated biblical interpretation with systematic doctrinal reflection, drew upon the philosophical tools that were common to their day, and kept the church's worship and social ethics in view. Many do the same today.

A final approach has no school dedicated to it, nor is there a widely used term for naming it. I call it *intentionally contextualized.*

Intentionally Contextualized Approaches to Theology

Intentionally contextualized approaches perform theology by emphasizing and leveraging the particular embodied perspectives of individual theologians. This may include one's nationality, race, gender, social location at the margins of society, sexual orientation, disability, and so on. Such approaches are "self-consciously partial and particular theologies, deliberately adopting standpoints previously marginalized or excluded in 'mainstream' theology, and hence drawing attention to the limitations of the mainstream itself."[11] Highly contextualized approaches overlap the others, such as biblical theology or systematic theology, but they intentionally and without apology arise *from* and speak *to* a specific social or political context.

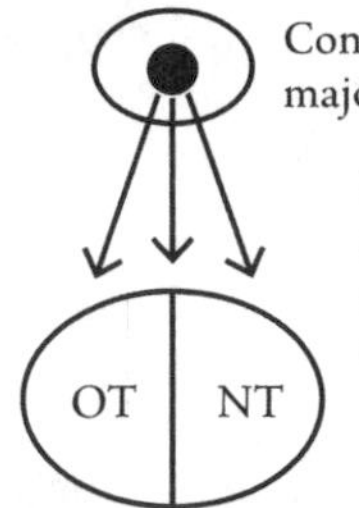

Context: nationality, race, gender, majority or minority culture, etc.

Biblical theology from explicitly contextualized approaches include African, Asian, and other non-Western commentaries, as well as feminist, disability, and post-colonial perspectives.

Please do not misunderstand: *all* theology is contextual – all the time and unavoidably. Theology arises in a particular setting and among a particular people. It always has its "feet" on the ground somewhere. People receive the teaching of the apostles in a particular time and place and pass it on then and there. To bring this out in the diagrams, every arrow originates from a dot (•): a place in time and space.

Yet intentionally contextualized approaches differ from theology in general by paying heightened attention to the bodily, political, or economic contexts of the theologian and her community. In my experience, those who think context matters little for theology tend to belong to the majority, privileged culture. Those on the margins know differently.

Forms of Theology

Theology is practiced according to many approaches, and it takes many *forms.* The specific task of theology in a particular moment often influences its form. The apostle Paul wrote letters because letter writing was an effective way to reach distant audiences. Gregory of Nazianzus wrote treatises to leaders of the early church, but he also wrote poetry so laypeople could grasp his theology.[12] A similar intent compelled Martin Luther to transform drinking songs from local pubs into Protestant hymns. In each case, the form suited the function. Historical settings also influence form. One setting may be suitable for one form, but in another setting the form is less effective. Here are ten forms of theology you may encounter.

Prayer

The first and primary response to God is prayer, and prayers are always theological. Sometimes prayers are written down so they can be prayed again and along with other Christians. The best examples of theology as prayer are found in the Psalms, in Jesus's teaching, and in the letters of the New Testament. All are theology in the form of prayers that were meant to be prayed over and over again. And in praying them, the theology embedded in the prayer becomes our own.

Prayers are *theology turned Godward.* This form of theology invites the reader into the author's personal experience of dialogue with God. We are invited to consider how our own theology shapes our language for God and to God. I once read that studying theology is not intended to make us cleverer but to shape and conform our prayers and praise to the truth of God revealed in Christ.[13] Theology as prayer reminds us that the language and ideas theology works with are ultimately in service to our relationship with God.

System of Doctrine

Many books assigned in college and seminary theology classes take this form (for better or for worse). All such works are distant echoes of Origen of Alexandria's *On First Principles* (third century), Thomas Aquinas's *Summa Theologica* (thirteenth century), and Philip Melanchthon's *Loci Communes* (sixteenth century), even as they may look different in language, style, and tone.

In a system of doctrine, an author arranges Christian teachings around headings such as "God," "Creation," or "Christology" and then tries to show the organic relationships between them. If we pay attention, the ordering of doctrines and even how the author names them can tell us quite a lot about the architecture.

Consider the following two works that bear the same name but whose ordering and layout reveal basic differences about the priorities and commitments of their authors: Friedrich Schleiermacher's *The Christian Faith* (nineteenth century) and Michael Horton's *The Christian Faith* (twenty-first century). In each case the theologian gives a systematic presentation of Christian teaching, and we find many of the same doctrines in both: Christology, the divine attributes, the church, the Trinity, and so on. But if you apply your architect's eye for theology – that is, if you try to do more than say, "Huh, concrete" – then you start noticing differences. I'll point out just one.

In Schleiermacher's *The Christian Faith*, the space is given shape and order by something he calls "Religious Self-Consciousness." By this he means our innate, common-to-all sense of God. To put it rather inelegantly, Schleiermacher starts his system with *our experience* then uses this principle all throughout the rest of the work as he moves toward God. If you followed this approach, where would you expect to find the doctrine of the Trinity? He places it last, the "coping stone" of Christian teaching, as he calls it.[14] Schleiermacher means that the Trinity is the doctrine that goes on top, resting on all that comes before it.

In Michael Horton's *The Christian Faith*, however, the architecture of the system is structured according to God's actions, rather than our experience of God. God's actions in history, Horton explains, "create the unfolding plot within which our lives and destinies find the proper coordinates."[15] The major sections of the work are thus titled "God Who Lives," "God Who Creates," "God Who Rescues," and "God Who Reigns in Grace." As we might expect (according to our architect's eye for theology), the doctrine of the Trinity is not the conclusion in Horton's work but the foundation – "not merely one doctrine among others" but the one that "structures all the faith and practice of Christianity."[16]

Order and arrangement in systems of doctrine are theological decisions. Train your eyes on the architecture. What is the overall effect? What is emphasized? What does the architecture communicate about Christian teaching as a whole? Don't be surprised if you notice themes drawn from biblical theology woven into the structure, such as "kingdom of God," "community," or "covenant." What do these tell you about the organizing principles of the work? Return often to the table of contents and read the introduction carefully; the theologian will often tell you what to look out for.

Treatise

Theology in this medium is often written to engage a crisis of belief or practice in the church through a carefully reasoned argument. *Against Heresies* by Irenaeus of Lyons (second century) is a good example, written to combat the teachings of early Gnostics. Another is Ulrich Zwingli's *On the Sacraments* (sixteenth century). Zwingli wrote during the upheavals of the Protestant Reformation. He wanted to set apart his views of the sacraments from those of the Roman Church and other Protestant Reformers.

Treatise theology is always situational. It responds to a specific issue or opportunity. Therefore, the focus of most treatises is relatively narrow and the tone is often polemical or even volatile. Keep reminding yourself of its narrow focus, and pay attention to how this influences the author's use of Scripture and other sources.

We should pause here and be honest: encountering theology in treatise form can be difficult and disorienting, and many new readers have the same experience with systems of doctrine. Do not feel bad. How many of us read carefully argued treatises in our free time, much less evaluate the relationships between various Christian doctrines?

The same sense of disorientation meets us in certain architectural spaces. Some architects create spaces so foreign to us that when we enter them we feel disoriented and uncomfortable. We look around but can't find our bearings. We might even feel afraid, small, and lost. A similar effect may grip us in small, cramped spaces.

I repeatedly see similar responses to theology with new students. Midway through their first semester, students sit in my office and say, "I don't know how to make heads or tails of this!" They feel lost and out of place in the readings. Consider the following quote. It's not from a beginning student. In fact, he holds a PhD in systematic theology and still feels lost in the theological space he describes. "Reading [Sergius] Bulgakov's pneumatology is like walking into a rich and ornate cathedral: one is immediately captured by the grandeur of its aesthetic beauty, but one easily gets lost in its wide expanses. The nuances of the architecture are often disorienting, which is a feeling I had repeatedly while reading."[17]

I had the same experience years ago while completing my PhD. I was reading a new theologian, and the book's title led me to expect a familiar space. How wrong I was! I remember describing the experience to my supervisor in architectural terms: "I'm reading theology, but I feel like I'm in the wrong room!" Its architecture was entirely foreign to me, and it frustrated and discouraged me. "Why can't I find my way around?" My doctoral supervisor smiled and told me to *keep reading*. "Be patient," he said, "Don't give up. Pay attention to what he's doing and not just what he's saying." I did, and he was right. Without knowing it, I was developing an architect's eye for theology. I was learning to read theology as inhabitation.

I never grew to enjoy that particular space. What Friedman writes about architecture I found to be equally true of some theology: "Appropriate scale enhances a sense of comfort with our surroundings. . . . Disproportionate scale, on the other hand, can make us feel out of place and uncomfortable."[18] The scale of some theology feels disproportionate; as if it wasn't made for humans to live in it. The effect is sometimes intentional, and other times (I fear) it occurs because the space was not constructed with readers/inhabiters in mind. "Every building or space has its characteristic sound of intimacy or monumentality, invitation or rejection, hospitality or hostility," Pallasmaa writes.[19] Some architecture, like some theology, never feels hospitable.

In most cases, however, the sense of disorientation recedes over time. Gradually, we learn to inhabit the books we read. Be patient. Don't give up.

Letter

Letters are written to particular people in a particular time and place. Like treatises, they are *situational*. The apostles wrote letters to various churches, helping them clarify their belief in Christ as other teachings competed for acceptance. In letters, theology is applied to everyday challenges like marriage, family, and politics. As a form of theology, letter writing continues in the modern church, as illustrated by the letters of the Nazi-resister Dietrich Bonhoeffer and the civil rights crusader Martin Luther King Jr. Email has the potential to serve a similar function. We mostly use it for quick, business-oriented communication, but I've had experiences with former students and pastors in which the medium was no less a vehicle for theology than letters.[20]

Remember that a letter (or an email) is situational. Its writer applies theology to specific issues facing particular people. Inhabiting this form is greatly served by engaging the world behind the page. Who is the author? What situation did she address? What challenge did she or her audience face?

Sermon or Homily

The sermon, or homily, is probably the most common form of theology, aside from prayer. Every week Christians use spoken sermons for biblical interpretation, theological insight, and exhortation. Some preach from notes, others more conversationally, but theology takes shape in and through them all. Most contemporary preaching bears little resemblance to the classic sermons of John Chrysostom (fourth century), Jonathan Edwards (eighteenth century), or Charles Spurgeon (nineteenth century), but sermons still engage in theology when they attempt to speak God's word to God's people in the present moment.

Like treatises and letters, preaching is *situational.* Theology as preaching is practiced in the midst of the gathered community of faith. Theology is spoken by a person in time and space and toward other Christian persons in time and space. The world behind this form of theology is, as for other forms, intensely informative as we seek to encounter the preacher's world of meaning.

Commentary on Scripture

Commentary on Scripture is not a medium in which Christians expect to find theology (at least not today). Since the eighteenth century, a clear line has separated theology from biblical interpretation. For most of Christian history, however, theology and biblical interpretation were inextricably wedded. Before it became common to study Scripture "academically" in the university, the primary audience for commentary was the church. St. Augustine's commentary on John (fifth century), Martin Luther's commentary on Galatians (sixteenth century), and Karl Barth's commentary on Romans (twentieth century) all bring theology to life through biblical interpretation.

Creed, Confession, or Catechism

In ecumenical creeds and confessions affirmed by denominations, Christians make concise statements of belief, often in response to challenging historical circumstances that demand clarity about doctrine. The main concern of such documents is *what* Christians believe (that Jesus is divine and human, and that his kingdom shall never end, etc.), not *how* such beliefs are so. Catechisms, on the other hand, focus on training young believers and often follow a question-and-answer format.

Those who write theology in this form express what lies at the heart of Christian faith, that which "has been believed everywhere, always, by all" (as Vincent of Lérins put it in the fifth century).[21] The early creeds of Nicaea and Chalcedon, for instance, were written because such beliefs were under attack. Crafting the shared language of the creed was like shoring up the defenses of a castle. Understanding the creeds requires that we read their architecture so that we can discern the "arrows" left for us. As we discussed in chapter 3, theologians leave arrows for their readers to follow: words, grammar, rhetoric, approach, and so on. Because creeds arise in the turmoil of conflict, we are greatly helped by following the pathway *behind* the page: the historical situation in which they were composed, the issues that gave rise to them, and the groups who composed them. For instance, the Nicene Creed (325) emphasizes Christ's divinity because that was under debate. Christ's humanity was not disputed, so little is said of it. The situation changed for the Council of Chalcedon (451). Read that creed and you find a clear expression of Christ's authentic human nature because it was under debate.

The same connection to a historical setting applies to confessions. They provide Christians with a sense for how faith can be "confessed" in their time and place. They often arise when Christians need to reaffirm essential convictions. Confessions are vehicles for Christians in particular times and places to say what is most essential about the Christian life. We can understand the flurry of Protestant confessions following the reformations of the sixteenth century, given their need to comprehend a new sense of what it means to be Christian. Or, more recently, the Belhar Confession (1982) was composed in post-Apartheid South Africa to emphasize racial reconciliation. Since racism remains with us, their confession challenges us to see as the Christians of South Africa saw and then live accordingly. "These historical confessions have provided Christians with a place to stand firm," writes pastor and theologian Philip Reinders, "but they also give us a place to humbly kneel."[22]

Poetry

Poetry uses figurative language to point readers toward truths than cannot be expressed in words. This makes poetry well suited to theology, because it resonates with and even accentuates the basic Christian claim that words fail to fully express our knowledge of God. Gregory of Nyssa (fourth century), Hildegard of Bingen (twelfth century), Phillis Wheatley (eighteenth century), Rowan Williams (twenty-first century), and so many others use poetry — like the psalmists of the Bible — to creatively and suggestively convey theology. Consider Hildegard's poem on the Trinity, in which she voices the mystery of God's triune nature:

> You are music.
> You are life.
> Source of everything,
> creator of everything,
> angelic hosts sing your praise.
> Wonderfully radiant,
> deep,
> mysterious. . . .[23]

Poetic theology often takes shape in hymns or other worship songs, as we see with the hymns of Ephrem the Syrian (fourth century) and Venantius Fortunatus (sixth century) and the spirituals of enslaved people in America (seventeenth–nineteenth centuries). All are poetic theology put to music.

Theology in poetic form points *off* the page. When you read poetic theology, allow it to suggest and evoke rather than explain. Beauty rarely explains so much as it sparks the imagination or moves us to a state of wonder and longing.

Autobiography or Memoir

Autobiography and spiritual memoir also carry theology. St. Augustine of Hippo (fifth century) wrote *The Confessions*, Catherine of Siena her

Dialogue (fourteenth century), and Old Elizabeth her *Memoir of Old Elizabeth, a Coloured Woman* (nineteenth century). In the twentieth century, spiritual and theological memoirs became very common. C. S. Lewis's *Surprised by Joy* and Kathleen Norris's *The Cloister Walk* are notable examples. Because theology has to do with God *and* the Christian, these forms are especially well suited as vehicles for theology.

Theology as autobiography is situated *in* the writer's encounter with God. This architectural space can transport us into intimate living room meetings to share the author's experience of God. Sometimes, we may find ourselves shaken by the author's portrait of faith when it differs from ours. The great advantage of the form is its deep connection to lived life, as in Anne Lamott's *Traveling Mercies*: "My coming to faith did not start with a leap but rather a series of staggers from what seemed like one safe place to another."[24] And in Thomas Oden's *A Change of Heart*: "As I worked my way through the beautiful, long-hidden texts of classic Christianity, I reemerged out of a maze to once again delight in the holy mysteries of the faith and the perennial dilemmas of fallen human existence. . . . I was deeply moved."[25] When you read autobiographical theology, allow the author's story of faith to raise questions and open new vistas as you reflect on your own faith story.

Fiction

Fiction is not a medium of theology most students are asked to engage (sadly). This is ironic, considering Jesus's extensive use of parables. Although characters and plot are invented, fiction can memorably say *true things* about God and the world. Jesus proved this time and again in his teaching. He doesn't expect us to believe in the historical reality of the prodigal son parable (Luke 15) – as if the father's house and the "far country" can be found on a map. That's not how parables work. Jesus taught through parable to depict *truly* our deep need for God and God's extravagant, relentless love for us. Fiction as theology likewise asks the reader to consider how the story imagines the world and the world in relation to God.

As theology, C. S. Lewis's *Chronicles of Narnia* resemble Jesus's parables. The reader can imagine God in these stories because he is written into the narrative. He stalks the land of Narnia as the mighty lion, Aslan (we find something similar with the character of Elyon in Ted Dekker's *Circle Trilogy*). For other authors, however, the work doesn't carry theology by portraying God in the narrative. Rather, they invent worlds in which we can vividly imagine the God of the gospel. Gary Schmidt's Newberry Honor book *The Wednesday Wars* and Marilynne Robinson's *Gilead*, *Home*, and *Lila* come to mind.[26]

Visual Art

We mustn't forget theology's *visual* forms. Christians have always sought to express their theology through carvings, mosaics, and icons.[27] Ancient and modern worship spaces are often covered in frescos and mosaics. The examples are so numerous, it's hard to know where to begin.

In the Western tradition, a few of my favorite theological artists are Masaccio (fifteenth century), Rembrandt van Rijn, and Michelangelo Merisi da Caravaggio (both seventeenth century). Check them out, and you'll see how each conveys deep theological truths on canvas. These are representational artists, so we find realistic scenes that we quickly relate to, but theology can take visual form even in nonrepresentational styles. We find this in the art of Makoto Fujimura (twenty-first century). Contemporary visual media also marry images with words, as in YouTube videos, films, and television shows.

Visual forms don't always incorporate words, but they still demand *interpretation*. Reading theology as inhabitation extends to theology in all its forms — even those we don't read in the usual way. Perhaps films and television series featuring long narrative arcs confront us most powerfully of all. We can inhabit these visual spaces just as we do written spaces.

Modes of Theology

Approaches are the methods of theology. Forms are the shapes of theology. Theology also has three distinctive *modes*: worship, witness, and critique.[28] The modes of theology entail the author's *intentions*, her particular *audience*, and the *goal*s for which she composed it. Look closely and you discover that authors make theological spaces – much as architects make buildings – for different groups of people and in order to nurture different kinds of experiences.

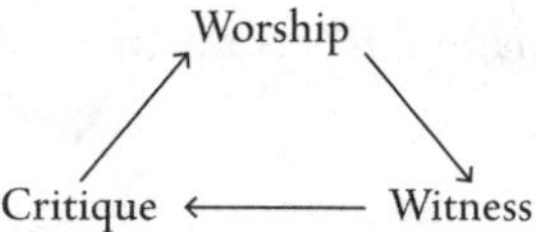

Worship

Theology begins as worship, or "doxology." At its most basic and primal, theology springs out from astonished awareness of God's ravishing goodness in Jesus Christ, leading us to cry, "Jesus is Lord!" Michael Horton expresses this response so well: "We find ourselves dumbfounded by God's grace in Jesus Christ, surrendering to *doxology* (praise). Far from masters, we are mastered; instead of seizing the truth, we are seized by it, captivated by God's gift, to which we can only say, 'Amen!' and 'Praise the Lord!'"[29] Theology begins as worship, and healthy theology turns us back toward worship in order to express the infinite riches of God's grace, mercy, and love. We might say that theology in the mode of worship is less about making arguments or building cases than increasing the breadth, depth, and height of the church's awareness of God. It strives to evoke "a fullness of vision."[30]

Naturally, the audience for worship-driven theology is the church, the people of God. The forms are then discrete practices embedded within the church's overall pattern of worship: the singing of hymns, for example, or the practice of joining together in corporate prayer.

Preaching functions as a particularly important form of theology-as-worship in the Western church, while the veneration of icons is a defining trait of the Orthodox East. It will be clear from these examples that theology in the mode of worship is usually linked to Christian worship spaces (i.e., the sanctuary), but this mode may also be found in worship-related texts. The Psalms provide the most obvious example, but doxology occasionally shines through texts that are conceptually dense and rigorous in argument. When the apostle Paul cites a hymn of praise to Christ in Philippians 2, his theology has shifted into the mode of worship.

Although we may think praise and thanksgiving are the only responses to worship theology, we would be wrong. Some theology in this mode does indeed lead to praise, but other instances instruct or even deconstruct us. Worship theology is occasionally prophetic. The sermons of Martin Luther King Jr., for example, bring light to the worshiping community by laying us bare and leaving us exposed to the force of God's justice.[31] In this way, King's preaching aims to replicate the effect that John's Revelation must have had two thousand years ago. When the text of Revelation reached the church in Ephesus, the congregation would have heard these searing words read aloud in worship: "I hold this against you: You have forsaken the love you had at first. Consider how far you have fallen! Repent and do the things you did at first. If you do not repent, I will come to you and remove your lampstand from its place" (Rev. 2:4–5). Surely those early believers felt laid bare and exposed by the truth. The response God sought from those prophetic words was transformed lives.

Witness

Worship theology has a hidden risk: we may forget that God means for the doors of the church to swing wide open to the unbelieving world. If theology remains *only* for the believing community – fueling and serving its imagination and worship – then it stagnates, always. It may fuel our missional activity, as King's sermons do, but in the mode of worship the theologian has not yet communicated directly to a watching world. Awareness of this risk is essential. Theology must move from worship to *witness*. In this mode, theology is for neighbors. The theologian seeks to commend the gospel to others and to persuade, to show its beauty and worth in ways that people outside the church can understand. Witness theology is found on the lips of Jesus when he commends himself to a Samaritan woman (John 4:26) or when he speaks of truth with Pilate (John 18:37). Paul moves into this mode when he speaks on the Areopagus to the gathered intellectuals: "People of Athens! I see that in every way you are very religious" (Acts 17:22). Because theology-as-witness is confident in the gospel's truth, it will courageously employ whatever cultural resources lie ready at hand.

If theology-as-witness is everywhere in the Christian tradition, perhaps it is because the church is always surrounded by those who have yet to believe, and the doors of our churches are always being flung wide by the Holy Spirit, drawing us out into lives of witness.

We find witness theology in the writings of the second-century apologists and theologians Tertullian and Justin Martyr, who appealed to Roman governors on behalf of early Christians. "Witness" describes the letter-writing campaign of sixteenth-century writer Argula von Grumbach, who spoke out against the imprisonment and torture of a young believer by the supposedly Christian civil authorities. The nineteenth-century theologian Friedrich Schleiermacher also practices witness theology, appealing to the educated skeptics of Christianity in *On Religion: Speeches to Its Cultured Despisers*. Today we find this mode at work in the public theology of Miroslav Volf, the award-winning fiction of Marilynne Robinson, the filmmaking of Scott Derrickson, the weekly newspaper column of theologian Amy Hall, and (potentially) in the conversations you have over the fence with your next-door neighbor. Approaches and forms vary, but this much remains constant: theology in the mode of witness is always pitched *toward* and *for* unbelieving neighbors.

Critique

In the mode of critique, we take stock of what worship and witness theology have brought forth. We ask, "Is this still the gospel?" For example, a worship leader evaluates a church's repertoire of songs to see if it expresses what the church believes about Jesus's death and resurrection; this is critical theology. A missionary considers her efforts to communicate the gospel in a foreign culture to see if contextualizing the gospel compromises the gospel's center; this is critical theology.[32] A denominational working group evaluates its stance on issues related to gender and sexuality; this, too, is critical theology.

Critical theology may also be a book, with the word "theology" on the spine or cover or not. Between its covers, the author forges a contemporary restatement of the Christian faith to correct missteps or errors in her time and place, as Christians do in every generation. Theologian-prophets come to mind, such as Miguel De La Torre (*Burying White Privilege*) and Soong-Chan Rah (*Prophetic Lament*), but even when the theological work doesn't have that in-your-face effect, it can still be critical theology, as we find in William Placher's *The Domestication of Transcendence* or Sarah Coakley's *God, Sexuality, and the Self*.[33] The main thing is this: in the mode of critique, the theologian invites us to see as she sees in order to *reform* and *renew* the church's witness and worship.

In the critical mode, the theologian seeks to be accountable to the sources of theology. She slows down, gathers others, and then prayerfully attends (again) to God's revelatory presence in the sources of theology. Rowan Williams offers a memorable phrase for theology in this mode: "Nagging at fundamental meanings."[34] He means that we should never grow so confident in ourselves and in our accumulated theology that we grow unwilling to be "nagged" – bothered, reminded, called back to awareness again – about the basic, fundamental, handed-down truths of our faith.

What Happens When Theology "Fails"?

What happens when theology fails? That is, what happens when the language of worship breaks down and we are not able to voice the content of our faith? What happens when the cultural assets at our disposal in evangelism seem to make the gospel opaque, or when critical theology cannot generate the linguistic, conceptual, or practical resources we desire? What happens when theology leads into *silence*?

I put the question this way in order to address a common expectation among beginning theology students: *theology should answer all my questions.* When theology does not offer the complete picture, when questions linger even after all the arguments have been considered, when things are less tidy than I desire, then theology must have failed, right?

Perhaps there is another way to approach this. Could it be that our perception of failure reveals that the expectation of a complete picture was wrong from the start?

The truth is that theology never reveals the *complete* picture we may desire. Sooner or later we must recognize that our ways of speaking about God are inadequate. However rich our worship theology, it can't fully express God's beauty and glory. However contextualized our witness theology, it can't sufficiently express the depths of the gospel or the mystery of human existence. No matter how diligently we apply our critical skills, theology-as-critique always produces a sketch rather than a finished portrait. Why is this?

When critical theology reaches its apex, we are thrown back upon the object toward *whom* theology was directed all along: the infinite, ineffable, holy, Living God, who is never fully captured by our descriptions, concepts, or language. As the fourth-century theologian Hilary of Poitiers wrote,

> Let imagination range to what you may suppose is God's utmost limit, and you will find Him present there; strain as you will there

> is always a further horizon towards which to strain. Infinity is His property, just as the power of making such effort is yours. Words will fail you, but His being will not be circumscribed. . . . Gird up your intellect to comprehend Him as a whole; He eludes you. God, as a whole, has left something within your grasp, but this something is inextricably involved in His entirety. . . . Reason, therefore, cannot cope with Him, since no point of contemplation can be found outside Himself and since eternity is eternally His.[35]

The silence of theology causes despair and fear for many. Does that resonate with you? I've seen it time and time again. For some, the insufficiency of theological language leads to a fear of deception: "Maybe we've been duped all along; the Christian faith is a lie!" Others despair over their own insufficiencies: "I must not be up to the task, not fit for theology."

When I teach theology, we inevitably reach a point at which theology's apparent failure confronts us. Our study leads us into silence. It always happens. The moment may arise while carefully attending to God's triune nature, as the language and conceptual resources available to us don't seem to say all that we want. So many "how" questions are left hanging. Or, it may confront us when giving our attention to Jesus's incarnation, and how it is that the church confesses him as being authentically and completely divine and human without remainder or contradiction. How can this be so? It doesn't seem theology has the resources available to say all that we want. Or, silence may come about when we contemplate the tenacity of evil in God's good world. We feel its weight and wish for answers and resolution. Yet evil persists. Where are you, God?

In these moments, I have found that the following story helps me offer the perspective my students need.

The first-century rabbi Akiva spent his time poring over Scripture in his quiet study, removed from the hustle and bustle of the market. Then, suddenly and to the surprise of all, he burst into the market *dancing*! How undignified, even strange. Why was he dancing? Eventually someone's desire overcame their discomfort, probably a child. He plucked up his courage, approached the dancing Akiva, and asked, "Rabbi, why are you dancing?" His answer may surprise you, especially if you've believed that theology will always provide the answers you desire. Akiva said, "I was studying the Torah and found something I don't understand!" Wait, what?!

Akiva found a mystery, a gaping expanse in his comprehension, but he didn't worry, doubt, or despair. He danced. Colliding with the limits of his knowledge, he didn't collapse into a crisis of faith. He danced. Pressing into the Scriptures to understand God, Akiva discovered his speechlessness, but he didn't fear the revelation of his weakness; he didn't fear the silence.

He danced.

Theology sometimes "fails" in the sense that it leads into silence, and that silence can lead us back to worship. So, if you're the dancing type, get up and dance! God is so great that he can't be fully comprehended! Any god we could entirely comprehend would never be worthy of our worship. Our great God surpasses our intellectual grasp, so dance!

But what about nondancers like me, and perhaps you? Thankfully, worship isn't restricted to dancing (whew!). For me, the silences of theology generate a quiet, awestruck reverence. I'm more naturally moved toward contemplation than dancing, and contemplation is *no less* fitting than dancing as worship. In the words of the psalmist, "My heart is not proud, LORD, my eyes are not haughty; I do not concern myself with

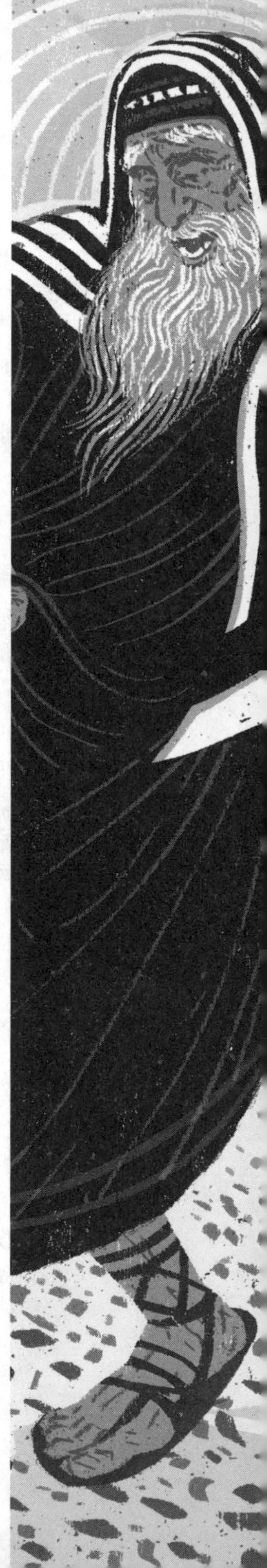

great matters or things too wonderful for me. But I have calmed and quieted myself, I am like a weaned child with its mother; like a weaned child I am content" (Ps. 131:1–2). Not dancing, but still worship.

Theology sometimes leads into silence, which can then lead us back to worship. We may get up and exuberantly dance, or we may sit down in awestruck silence, or — *perhaps you've been waiting for this because neither of those responses names your experience yet* — we can also crumple in lament. Modern worship seldom includes lament, but it just might be the only honest form of worship in the face of some silences. How else, but through lament, can we move honestly and transparently *toward* God in the face of great human suffering? "O my people, trust in him at all times. Pour out your heart to him, for God is our refuge" (Ps. 62:8 NLT). Lament is worship that acknowledges our pain before God in the face of incomprehensible suffering or confusion.

When our confusion is dark and persistent, lament *persists* with God. It says, in effect, "God, I'm in the deepest, darkest hole. I can't see a way out. I can't see you." It admits that we have no answers, that we are prone to exhaust our own strength: "I am worn out from my groaning" (Ps. 6:6). The book of Psalms overflows with such prayers.[36] "In lament we are confused, angry, and grieving people," Todd Billings writes in the midst of his battle with incurable cancer. But the Psalms teach us that we are not just that:

> We have been given the script of the Psalms for playing our part in the drama: we are confused, angry, and grieving people who have been given the privilege of crying out to the Lord as his covenant people. Indeed, we are actors who have been clothed with Christ by the Spirit in the theater of God's drama. Because of this, we can openly admit our confusion, anger, and grief without worrying that it will be the last word about who we are.[37]

Here is the question that presses on us at this moment: What must be true of us in order that theology's apparent "failures," and the silences we have been speaking of, lead us not to fear or to despair but to some form of worship that fits our needs and circumstances?

Let me offer this. It is not the whole picture, of course, but it's near the center of what I believe. We must be the kind of readers who are so *at home with God* that we are not afraid of all that we cannot control. We're frailer that we like to admit. Refrains of fear ring in our ears. Our environments, our communities, our inner lives are raucous and disordered. Our power brings us less control than we wish. These uncomfortable truths intrude into our theology, causing the silences to evoke dismay, anxiety, and fear. We want to "inhabit a territory that is clearly defined and capable of being defended. *We need to know where we are.*"[38]

I should remind you, dear reader, that even when our picture is incomplete or not as tidy as we wish, we know *where* we are and *whose* we are. As the adopted children of the triune God, we share through the Holy Spirit in the Father's and Son's love for each other (John 17:20–26). We're at home already, even as we wait for the fulfillment of our at-home-ness (Rom. 8:22–25)! As we learn to live more authentically in this truth, we will find that theology's silences are moments for worship. For some, it will look like joyous, raucous, undignified dancing; for others, feelings of reverent awe. For others still, the truest worship arising out of theology's silence will be honest, agonized lament. The Living God with whom we are already at home is so great that each form of worship can be a fitting response.

Prayer

Boundless God,
You are always beyond us.
  For us,
  yes,
  but beyond us.
Forgive us for forgetting that you are God.

Forgive us for fearing the silences of our unknowing.
Forgive us for having so little faith that even in our unknowing
you are still God.
For us,
yes,
but beyond us.
Let us not be afraid: Calm our fears, heavenly Father.
Let us not be afraid: Reassert your presence, Lord Jesus.
Let us not be afraid: Enable us beyond our control, Holy Spirit,
to trust that you are still God.
For us,
yes,
but beyond us. Amen.

Summary

The world *of* theology entails its architecture. Architecture is the way theology's sources are brought together to build the shape we inhabit as readers. Our architect's eye develops as we learn to identify the different approaches of theology, the many different forms of theology, and the different modes. The three modes of theology are worship, witness, and critique. Theology will always seem to fail in the critical mode, for it will run into the limitations of language and concepts to reckon with the Living God. Our response should be, given the object of theology, not despair but dancing, reverence, or even lament — that is, worship.

Questions for Reflection and Discussion

1. To which of theology's approaches are you most naturally drawn? Why do you suppose that is?
2. If you could choose among any of theology's forms presented in this chapter, which would you choose to read? Which would you most likely avoid? What lies behind those reactions?

3. How did you react to Akiva's dancing? Was his response to divine mystery inspiring or bothersome or something else? How is it different from or similar to your typical response to mystery?

Theology Lab: Write a Collect

"Sovereign Lord," they said, "you made the heavens and the earth and the sea, and everything in them. . . . Stretch out your hand to heal and perform signs and wonders through the name of your holy servant Jesus."

— *Acts 4:24, 30*

The whole purpose of theological education [is] not simply to make students cleverer, but to help them learn better ways to speak to God in prayer, and to one another in witness. . . . In this way, scholarly discipline becomes a form of discipleship; theology becomes an exercise in prayer.

— *Ben Myers*[39]

Writing collect prayers forms us to approach theological reading in relation to prayer, which is fundamental to Christian life. Nothing is more basic to the Christian life than prayer, so reading theology — whatever else it might be — should be related to our active dialogue with God.

Writing collect prayers and praying them in corporate worship is an ancient practice (the "o" is pronounced as in *pollen* and the emphasis falls on the first syllable). When collect prayers are written and prayed based on theological readings, we are trained to make connections between reading and our Christian lives.

In worship, collect prayers are used for adoration, invocation, confession, illumination, and dedication. Collect prayers have several parts:

Address: statement of address to God (Almighty God . . .)
Acknowledgment: description of God in terms of a specific attribute or action (. . . to you all hearts are open, all desires known, and from you no secrets are hid . . .)
Petition: request for God to act (. . . cleanse the thoughts of our hearts by the inspiration of your Holy Spirit . . .)
Aspiration: declaration of our desire for a particular result (. . . that we may perfectly love you and worthily magnify your holy name . . .)
Pleading: acknowledgment of the one who mediates our prayers (. . . through Jesus Christ our Lord, Amen).

The collect form mirrors the pattern of Acts 4:23–40, where acknowledging God's creation of heaven and earth leads the one praying to plead with God to act in power *again*: "Stretch out your hand to heal and perform signs and wonders through the name of your holy servant Jesus."

When writing a collect based on a theological reading, we look for ways, first, to acknowledge who God is or what God has done. Then we plead with him to be and act accordingly in our lives today. My students write and pray collect prayers in preparation for every class. Holly describes the benefit of doing so:

> What took place was a giving back to God what I thought I had accomplished on my own. I had done the reading. I had answered the questions. I did the learning. But it is God who teaches. He enables me to learn. By praying my learning to him, I praise and acknowledge him for it. Grace encounters even my pride in my studies and begs me to be transformed; to acknowledge and worship God for everything in my life, including my studies.

The Anglican *Book of Common Prayer*, the Presbyterian *Book of Common Worship*, and the ecumenical *Worship Sourcebook* are full of good examples. Here are several collect prayers from my students to help you get started.

[*Based on a reading about God's providence*]
Almighty and Ever-living God, who sustains the world from beginning to end. You were there before the creation of the world in ages past, you will be there in the eschaton and consummation of history. We ask that you continually remind us that you are always here, right now, and that you have promised to share your presence with us until the end of the age. We pray these things in and through the name of Jesus Christ, who lives and reigns with you and the Holy Spirit, One God now and forever, Amen.

[*Based on a reading about the Son's incarnation*]
Dear Heavenly Father, maker of heaven and earth. We thank you for sending us your Holy Son, who was begotten of you from the beginning of time. That He may take on human form, living in the flesh as human as man but, still, fully divine. We ask that you would lead us daily to live our lives in an attempt to be as holy as your Son. To honor his death by giving our lives as a living sacrifice, holy and pleasing to you. That we may forfeit our earthly desires to live as your Son did. We ask this all in the name of our Lord Jesus Christ who lives and reigns with you and the Holy Spirit, one God, forever and ever. Amen.

[*Based on a reading about God's self-revelation*]
O gracious God who meets us at the horizon of our imagination and who resides in our midst of reality. Guide us in your ways. Shatter our mirrors that we mistake for windows. Burst our self-made claims of weak minds and scared hearts. Of these Lord we want to see You, only You. We want to go deep and discover the earth-shaking

whispers of your love which you've revealed from the beginning of creation. In your faithfulness hear our doxology to you. Father, may your Kingdom come, by the work of the Holy Spirit with your Son, Christ Jesus. Amen.

7

Invitations of Theology: In Front of the Page

> *At that time the kingdom of heaven will be like ten virgins who took their lamps and went out to meet the bridegroom. Five of them were foolish and five were wise.*
>
> — *Matthew 25:1–2*

> *What works of design and architecture talk to us about is the kind of life that would most appropriately unfold within and around them.*
>
> — *Alain de Botton*[1]

Everything leads to this.

Works of theology *project* a world and invite you, dear reader, to live as if it were true — to see as the author sees and to *live* accordingly.[2] "This is the way the world is in light of God," the author says to you. "Now go and live within that world. Live according to its truths and in harmony with its rhythms and patterns." Every part of the work is there to help you see as the author sees, and then to go and live.

This chapter has three parts. In the first, I illustrate the world in front with a sandcastle I once built with my daughters, a letter from the apostle Paul, and another letter from St. Ignatius of Antioch. Second, we take up the challenge of living in a world where rival visions of reality compete for our attention. What are we to make of their claims to represent the world *as it actually is*? We have skirted along the edges of this challenge throughout the book; now we face it head on. How do we take the risk of drawing so close to an author's projected world? The truth and beauty in her world of meaning must be separated from the errors and missteps. How do we love the author while exercising discernment? In part three of the chapter, I show how to navigate this challenge in terms of three wisdoms.

Part 1: Sandcastle City

Some years ago I made a sandcastle with my kids. "Where should the wall go, Dad?" my youngest daughter asked. We had decisions to make because our castle was turning into a city. I pondered the question about the wall for a moment and said, "Why do we need a wall?" She stopped packing sand into a bucket, and her older sister looked up. "I'm just saying," I continued, "this is *our* city. We can imagine it how we want. What if we built the way we hope cities could be and how we dream people could live together? Would *that* city have a wall?"

In the end, our sandcastle city didn't have a wall. Not because everyday cities don't or shouldn't have walls but because the city we hope for wouldn't. "It should make everyone want to come in," we decided. My daughters also positioned the power plant behind the hills so it wouldn't obstruct anyone's view. We arranged the houses on the plain in circles to increase contact with neighbors. On the hill, we formed houses *into* the slope rather than onto it, to preserve its natural form. What informed these decisions for us? Was it our time and place, our experiences, and Revelation's vision of God dwelling among us?[3] You bet.

Our sandcastle city had a world behind, of, and in front of it. The world *behind* our city included my kids and me, our experiences, the time in which we live, and our hope of God's new creation in his kingdom. This all enabled and limited our city, for we built what our imagination thought possible. The world *of* our city was the little sand structures themselves, their spatial arrangement, the absence of a wall, and so on. And all of those elements together projected an imagined world to anyone passing by — not a picture of what cities or castles actually look like but a *vision* of our hoped-for-city. A city without a wall spoke of our hope for inclusion, circular neighborhoods spoke of our desire for community, and the placement of homes on the hill spoke of our hope for buildings that respond to landscapes (we're nerds for architecture).

Would swimsuit-clad viewers catch all that, each of them occupying their own world in front? Probably not at a glance, but if one stopped and studied our city, and then imagined herself within it – everything a wise reader of theology would do – then she would see a possible world and a possible way of living.

Standing before our sandcastle city teaches us so much about reading theology as inhabitation because it shares the movement from comprehension to understanding and then to appropriation. Let's recall from chapter 3 how this works.

Comprehension always comes first. We seek to comprehend unfamiliar terms and concepts, or the forms of making an argument that are new to us. These intellectual achievements are like noting the absence of a wall in the sandcastle city or considering what it could mean to position the houses as we did. The missing wall and the houses (and all the rest of the sandcastle city) are the "arrows" we left for the swim-suited viewer. It's much the same when reading: the author leaves us arrows, and by following them we begin to *understand* what the work is really about (we engage in what I've called "encounter"). When reading, "to understand is to follow the dynamic of the work, its movement from what it says to that about which it speaks."[4]

A work of theology is *about* a vision of God and the world the reader is invited to see and live within. The work of theology projects that world and you, dear reader, meet that projected world in front of theology. Reading as inhabitation places us at the author's shoulder, looking at her projected world, considering her invitation to go and live within it. "See as I see," the author invites, "then go and live."[5]

Will I *appropriate* this world of meaning? Will I accept it as the way things are in truth? The stakes are low in a sandcastle city, but they are high for us as readers of theology. How we see God and the world in light of God dramatically shapes how we live. I will illustrate this with the work of two early Christians: the apostle Paul and St. Ignatius of Antioch.

The Apostle Paul

In Paul's letters to the churches in Rome and Ephesus, he first states what is *true* of us because of Christ, and then he unfurls how we should therefore *live*. Paul connects the projected world of union with Christ – what is true for us – with ways of living that follow from that state of being. Tracing Paul's verb tenses is one way to see this. In the first portion of the letters, we find verbs that identify states of being, called "indicative" verbs: "you *are*" or "we *are*." In the second portion, however, we find verbs that call for action, called "imperative" verbs: "remember" or "live" or "be careful." With Romans and Ephesians, Paul's use of tenses splits nearly down the middle. In Romans, for instance, Paul makes the turn at the beginning of chapter 12: "Therefore, I urge you, brothers and sisters, in view of God's mercy [*which was a major topic of the letter up to this point, described in the indicative*], to offer your bodies [*imperative!*] as a living sacrifice, holy and pleasing to God – this is your true and proper worship" (Rom. 12:1).

For Paul, encountering the reality of God's mercy in Christ leads to the discovery of a world projected for us – not just any world, but the *real* world, the world as it *actually* is. In the real world, there is simply no other way to live than to offer all of yourself to God. Such life is flourishing life. True life. Every reader since those first Christians in Rome encounters the same invitation to see and live in that projected world.

We find Paul making a similar move in Ephesians. Chapter 4 begins, "I urge you to live a life [*imperative!*] worthy of the calling you have received" (Eph. 4:1). Up to this point, the letter is entirely focused on describing the state of one's existence in union with Christ. Indicative verbs are everywhere in the first three chapters. Paul projects a world that he wants the reader to accept as her *true* world. What comes next is the imperative to live accordingly, we might say to "fit" ourselves into the world as it really is: "Follow God's example [*imperative!*], therefore, as dearly loved children, and walk in the way of love [*imperative!*], just as Christ loved us and gave himself up for us as a fragrant offering and sacrifice to God" (Eph. 5:1). Paul's verb tenses and the structure of his letters are arrows pointing toward the world he seeks to project and the right, fitting way of living in it. You are united to Christ – that is the world as it really is for you – so follow the pattern of that world and live along its grain: imitate Christ by living a life of love. Every Christian reader is now standing at Paul's shoulder, seeing as he sees and hearing his invitation to live accordingly.

C. S. Lewis says that seeing with an author is the real purpose for every sort of reading. "We want to see with other eyes," he writes, "to imagine with other imaginations, to feel with other hearts, as well as with our own." In doing so, "as in worship, in love, in moral action, and in knowing, I transcend myself; and am never more myself than when I do."[6] Lewis might as well have been talking about theology, because through every work of theology – including Paul's letters – the author invites us to see with her eyes.

To be sure, we read Paul's letters as inspired Scripture, eager for the Holy Spirit's encounter. The world of meaning that Paul projects is not just any world; it's the world as it really is. In that sense, Paul's letters are so unlike my daughters' sandcastle city and whatever theology we may read other than Holy Scripture. But in another sense, Paul's letters and the works of theology that draw upon Scripture as a source are very similar. As we inhabit works of theology as readers, moving through comprehension to understanding, we receive a common invitation: *see* as I see and then *live.*

Christian teaching about the Trinity centers on God's life in himself, but it also includes a vision of God's interactions with creatures and their possible ways of praying, loving, and being together. The doctrine of the *imago Dei* is not just about having been made in the image of God. To speak of that image implies a world of richer human relations to God, a vision of God himself, as well as possible ways of seeing human capacities, disabilities, and our telos or ultimate destination.[7] Similarly, Christian teaching about creation is never only about the divine origin of the world. If God made all that is, how are we to love and care for God's world? And what role does creation play within God's redeeming and sanctifying work?[8]

Works of theology are invitations to *see* and then – even when not stated explicitly – to *live*.

St. Ignatius of Antioch

Early Christians like Ignatius understood that our vision of Jesus shapes our life. I am not referring to obeying Jesus's teachings, such as loving your neighbors. Rather, our life is shaped by who we believe Jesus *is* – the nature of his person.

Ignatius was born just ten years after the crucifixion of Jesus. He would grow up to become the second bishop of the church in Antioch (present-day Syria) during the reign of Emperor Trajan (AD 98–117). For reasons unknown to us, Ignatius was sentenced to die in Rome. As he was being taken to Rome, Ignatius wrote letters to several churches. In these letters, Ignatius repeats a common theme: *Jesus was truly and authentically human*. This is deep indeed, but it isn't merely an abstract idea, something that can be filed away in the mind before going about business as usual. No, Jesus's true and authentic humanity is a major feature of the architecture of Christian theology. And for Ignatius, the theology of Christ's humanity projects a world and clarifies the way of living within it.

Notice how Ignatius praises his readers' firm belief in Christ's humanity, and how it informs their lives:

> I perceived that you are settled in unshakable faith, nailed, as it were, to the cross of our Lord Jesus Christ, *in flesh* and spirit . . . with full conviction with respect to our Lord that he is *genuinely of David's line* according to the flesh, son of God according to divine will and power, *really born of a virgin* and *baptized by John* that "all righteous-

> ness might be fulfilled" (Matt. 3:15) by him, *really nailed up in the flesh* for us.[9]

The message here is, "Well done, Smyrnaeans! You held onto the apostles' teaching that Jesus really is the Son of God and also the *Son of Man*. Bravo!" Notice, though, how Ignatius goes on to explain what happens when you cease to believe this. Those who deny Jesus's humanity, he writes, "have no regard for love; no care for the widow, or the orphan, or the oppressed; of the prisoner or the free; of the hungry, or of the thirsty. They stay away from the Eucharist and from prayer, because they do not admit that the Eucharist is the flesh of our Savior Jesus Christ, which suffered for our sins, and which the Father, by his goodness, raised up again."[10] Ignatius simply doesn't believe that your Christology (theology of Jesus) is a tidy set of ideas. No, it's a projected world and *a way of living*!

When you deny the humanity of Jesus, Ignatius reasons, then you find yourself caring little for the humanity of others. The needs of widows and orphans, the hungry and thirsty, these are tangible human needs. They are the stuff of our bodies. When the architecture of your Christology lacks a truly and authentically human Jesus, Ignatius argues, then your love will be deficient. Yes, your *love*. You cease caring about the poor and leave the hungry to starve.

Does Ignatius quote any of Jesus's many teachings about love? No. He isn't saying that some have forgotten Jesus's teachings. That would be easy enough to fix: "Be good Christians; obey Jesus's teachings!" No, Ignatius is addressing the world in front of Christology because he knows that our theology of Jesus — like our sandcastle city — projects a world and a way of *living*.

Part 2: Worlds in Competition

We are surrounded by sandcastle cities. They are the TV shows we consume, the movies we watch, the novels we enjoy, the billboards we see — and the works of theology we read. Each competes for our attention. Each projects a world for us to see as the *real* world. And each invites us to make our home there, to live along its grain, to follow its patterns. Michel de Certeau calls these projected worlds "narrativities" to remind us that each encapsulates a story about how things are. "The listener walks all day through a forest of narrativities, journalistic, advertising and televised, which, at night, slip a few final messages under the door of sleep. More than the God recounted to us by the theologians of the past, these tales have a function of providence and predestination: they organize our work, our celebrations – even our dreams – in advance."[11]

Part of the power of these stories comes from our lack of awareness; we don't realize they are inviting us to make our home in their projected world. We seldom ask the question constantly facing us, Which projected world will we accept as the real one? (In case someone tells you there isn't a real world to accept, don't believe them. That story is a projected world too!)

Ryan Murphy is the creative mind behind some of TV's most successful recent shows, such as *Glee*.[12] Asked to describe his job, he said, "I create worlds." He creates them intentionally – just as any maker of sandcastle cities would – to invite viewers into a possible way of seeing and living. "What I'm interested in doing now," he says,

> is to go and give voices that are not being heard a platform, and just sort of bring people into people's homes that you think you may hate or despise, but the truth of the matter is if you just sat in a room [with them] I think you would admire them and I think that you would have a lot more in common with them than you think. . . . *Maybe it will change one person's mind, and that's all I can aim for*.[13]

Every TV show, like every work of theology, opens a space for communication. It projects a possible world and way of living within it. As my oldest daughter once said after reading a novel, "It's so *true*, Dad!" "Wait," I asked, knowing full well what I was doing, "how can a novel be true?" She replied without hesitation, "It pictures how life *is* for a teenager." Exactly. That's the power of the world it projects. It intends to be the *real* world.

Will I live in this world? Reading theology culminates with choices. Having encountered an author's projected world – God and everything in light of God – the reader must decide, Will I live in this world? Will I live along its grain? Will I live according to its patterns? In literary theory, this choice is called "appropriation." Ricoeur likens it to playing a musical score. The metaphor helps us think about reading as an activity that ends with an active choice. It's one thing to read the score and altogether another to play it.

What will we *do* with what we've read? The metaphor of pilgrimage offers a similar emphasis on action, direction, and involvement of the whole self. It puts the question to me: Will I move in the directions of this journey? Will I order my steps according to the destinations and cadences that are fitting to this world? The point of appropriation is whether I will accept an author's vision of the world and live accordingly, not in theory but in practice. Will I *play* the score? Will I *join* the pilgrimage?

Appropriation may go in three directions. First, I may accept the world projected for me as, in fact, the real world and conform my life to it. I play the score; I join the pilgrimage; I live according to the patterns of this world. Second, I may reject it entirely. This world is simply false. Third, I may find areas of convergence and divergence between the world I know and the world projected for me. In other words, I may find areas of overlap and difference between the view of God and the world I bring to my reading of theology and the author's projected world. On the metaphor of musical harmony, between the projected world and mine, I find consonance and dissonance.

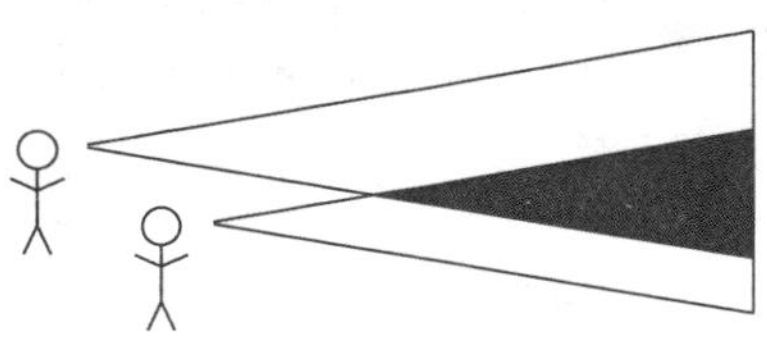

For Christians reading Christian theology, the third possibility is the most likely: consonance and dissonance, overlap and difference. After all, if the author is a sibling in Christ, and she constructed her discourse space from the sources of theology we share, then areas of overlap shouldn't surprise. This third option raises an important question: How do we *discern* convergence and divergence? How do we "tune our ears" to hear the consonance and dissonance? More urgently, how do we discern *truth* from error?

We need wisdom.

Part 3: Reading Theology Wisely

Wisdom is our developed ability to *perceive* correctly what stands in front of us, discern how to *respond*, and then actually *do* what the situation requires.[14] Jesus describes wisdom along these lines in his parable of the ten virgins:

> At that time the kingdom of heaven will be like ten virgins who took their lamps and went out to meet the bridegroom. Five of them were foolish and five were wise. The foolish ones took their lamps but did not take any oil with them. The wise ones, however, took oil in jars along with their lamps. The bridegroom was a long time in coming, and they all became drowsy and fell asleep. At midnight the cry rang out: "Here's the bridegroom! Come out to meet him!" Then all the virgins woke up and trimmed their lamps. The foolish ones said to the wise, "Give us some of your oil; our lamps are going out." "No," they replied, "there may not be enough for both us and you. Instead, go to those who sell oil and buy some for yourselves." But while they were on their way to buy the oil, the bridegroom arrived. The virgins who were ready went in with him to the wedding banquet. And the door was shut. (Matt. 25:1–10)

Jesus calls the virgins with oil wise because they correctly *perceived*, *discerned*, and *acted*. They assessed their situation: it may be a long time until the bridegroom arrives. They discerned the appropriate action: bring extra oil for our lamps. And, most importantly, they acted, performing the work of bringing oil.[15]

Jesus tells the parable so we would be *wise* about the time in which we live. Now is the time of God's in-breaking kingdom. We don't know the time of his return, so we must be ready. Those who are wise are the ones who correctly perceive the time (this is the time of the kingdom), discern an appropriate response (be ready for the King's return), and then actually do what's required. Be ready: trust Jesus as King, align your deepest self with him through faith, then follow his teachings! Be wise.

Regarding the many kinds of texts we read, Alan Jacobs writes, "Discernment is required to know what kind of gift one is being presented with, and in what spirit to accept it (if at all)."[16] Moving across the room and standing at the author's shoulder to receive the gift of their projected world does not necessitate accepting it as the way things are.

Three kinds of wisdom are required to discern whether we should *accept* the gift or *walk away*. The first wisdom is to follow time-tested rules. The second is to form the appropriate, hard-won, Spirit-formed virtues. The third wisdom is the hardest to name. It is the discernment to know that empathy is risky and the knack for responding appropriately.

Wisdom 1: Reading by the Rules

To discern truth from error, people (across the stretch of Christian history) have read theology according to four modest guides, or "rules." Readers outside the church would not accept these, but they are fundamental to Christians. Does this mean that Christians apply all of them in exactly the same way and give them equal priority in every case? No, yet across the long history of Christian faith and across different traditions today, we find these rules for discerning truth from error: the rule of Scripture, the rule of faith, the rule of love, and the rule of prayer.

The Rule of Scripture

Theologians look to Scripture as a source of God's self-revealing activity (see chapter 5). So, it would seem the reader only needs to determine if a theologian is using Scripture as a source for their view of God and everything in light of God. If only it were that simple! Scripture is and has been interpreted in different ways on many different topics. This is hardly new. Even Jesus experienced resistance to his interpretations. He interpreted Scripture for the Jews of his day so they would see him as Messiah, but many read the Scriptures differently. It brought him to tears (Luke 19). Likewise, the apostle Paul went from synagogue to synagogue, reasoning with the Jews from the Scriptures; some believed, others didn't. Where does that leave us related to the rule of Scripture?

Reading theology by the rule (or guide) of Scripture is like tracking the orbit of a celestial body in space. The body with the greatest mass pulls other objects into its orbit. It draws them around it and determines their direction. The rule of Scripture should be used with theology like that: how close is the "orbit" of this theology around Scripture? This attunes us as readers to pay attention to the author's use of Scripture and the influence it has, or doesn't have, on their claims (even as there are different ways to evaluate this).

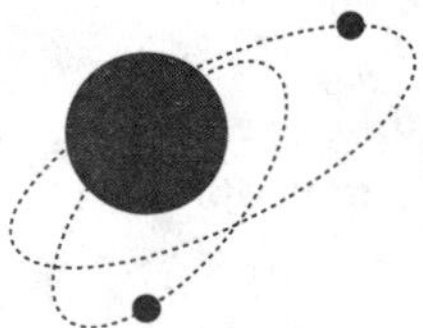

The rule of Scripture compels us to consider the author's "Scripture orbit." Every Christian's theological imagination follows some orbit around Scripture, even if they aren't aware. Like the author's, our Scripture orbit is influenced by our personal history, time and place, and by our particular communities of faith. Those communities include our local churches, our families, and our faith traditions (Protestant, Roman Catholic, Baptist, etc.).

When your Scripture orbit differs from the author, then divergences appear. You may discern that these differences compel you to reject the author's projected world. Or, they may signal that your Scripture orbit should change. To make such choices we need another rule to guide us.

The Rule of Faith

The earliest Christians discerned that Scripture wasn't enough for discerning truth from error in theology. It wasn't that Scripture was unimportant but that theologians on both sides of various debates could draw upon Scripture. The orbits were different, of course – those involved in the debates were making different claims from the same text – but they were in close orbit around Scripture nonetheless. They had to determine the answer to this question: What guides us when our interpretations of Scripture differ? Their answer was the rule of faith (Latin, *regula fidei*).

The rule of faith became a shared understanding of how the whole of Scripture should be interpreted according to the revelation of Jesus as Messiah. In the second century, St. Irenaeus likened the rule of faith to a key one uses when assembling a mosaic. To arrange the pieces correctly, you need a key. Here are the first few lines of the key or rule Irenaeus provides. He says the church receives this from the apostles: we believe "in one God, the Father Almighty, Maker of heaven, and earth, and the sea, and all things that are in them; and in one Christ Jesus, the Son of God, who became incarnate for our salvation; and in the Holy Spirit, who proclaimed through the prophets the dispensations of God."[17] Does this sound familiar?

The Apostles' Creed and the Nicene Creed are remarkably similar to what St. Irenaeus and others referred to as the rule of faith. As readers of theology, these creeds serve as our rule in the following way:

they keep before our eyes the central, most fundamental, most widely shared elements of our Christian faith.

Rule of Scripture ⟷ Rule of Faith

The rule of faith is not to be used instead of the rule of Scripture. Both rules are used together, held together, and each leads us to the other. The rule of Scripture leads to the rule of faith as we seek to discern the Bible's fundamental story. The other way around, the rule of faith leads us to the rule of Scripture because it's there we find God's ongoing revelation of himself through the words of the Bible.

The Rule of Love

Jesus was asked about the greatest commandment in Scripture, and he responded by giving two: love God with everything you are (heart, soul, mind, and strength), and love your neighbor as you would love yourself. Jesus went on to say that all the rest of Scripture "hangs" on these commands (Matt. 22:37–40). We should understand all Scripture according to these commands, or "through" these commands. They are the organizing principle of Scripture. Love God and love your neighbor. What does this have to do with theology?

Whatever else the world in front of theology might include, it should never lead the reader to love God or their neighbor *less*. The rule of love keeps before our eyes Jesus's summary of Scripture. It reminds us that however greatly we care about truth and error in ideas and doctrines – and we should – we must not forget that ideas and doctrines shape behavior. The rule of love compels us to ask, Does the world in front of this theology enable me to follow Jesus's teaching to love God with everything you are and love your neighbor as yourself?

St. Augustine applied the rule of love to interpreting Scripture. He acknowledged that we have many good and essential tools at our disposal for reading the Bible, such as knowledge of the original languages, grammar, and rhetoric. He advises we should make use of every one. However, according to Augustine, we can't say we understand any part of Scripture unless it leads us to *love God and others*: "So anyone who thinks that he has understood the divine scriptures or any part of them, but cannot by his understanding build up this double love of God and neighbor, has not yet succeeded in understanding them."[18] He's saying, "Fine, you say you understand this or that bit of the Bible, so show me your life. Is your so-called understanding causing you to love God and others? If not, you had better take another look at your reading of Scripture and at yourself. You may be the problem, not your interpretation." The rule of love applies to theology as well.

Reading theology by the rule of love compels us to imagine ourselves out there in front of the text with the author. If I were to live according to this author's world of meaning, would it lead me to love? If not, is that a problem with the author or with me? Is there, perhaps, something about me that needs to change?

The Rule of Prayer

Wise readers of theology pray, pray often, and pray like they mean it. It aligns our hearts with the work of God's Spirit in and through our lives, even as we read. Prayer is critical to cultivating the right posture toward authors and to opening ourselves to the Spirit's activity. The rule of prayer ensures that as we read our hearts remain aligned with the Holy Spirit and sure of ourselves as God's children. "The Spirit himself testifies with our spirit that we are God's children" (Rom. 8:16). We know whose we are and where we are.

As Christians, our deepest sense of identity comes through the Spirit's confirmation. The Spirit's confirmation of our true selves in Christ may come to us immediately, without any means at all, or it can come to us "mediately," through means at our disposal, such as study, catechesis, and training. The rule of prayer cultivates an attitude of prayerful attentiveness to God. Without it, all such means can devolve into dry intellectualism, image management, and pride. Through the rule of prayer, however, we join the prayers of the Son and the Spirit who ceaselessly pray on our behalf. While empathy places us at risk of losing ourselves in an author's false projected world, reading by the rule of prayer keeps drawing us back toward our true selves in Christ.

The rule of prayer also cultivates a spirit of love for the author that serves empathy. By empathy we mean something like "open-mindedness," but I've avoided the term for fear that it too easily evokes intellectualism. Reading as a living encounter is not less than intellectual, but it's so much more. It involves all that we are, because we always bring all that we are to the practice of reading, even if we don't realize it. We never cease being embodied persons even though we may downplay the fact. As philosopher Jason Baehr uses the word "open-mindedness," he very much describes what we've been talking about in terms of empathy. "The sort of open-mindedness that flows from Christian love," he writes,

> is not blind; it does not amount to an arbitrary or irrational casting of ourselves or our beliefs at the feet of our intellectual adversaries. Rather, it comes from a place of deep intellectual confidence and nearness to God. A person whose Christian beliefs, say, are not well-grounded or who in her "heart of hearts" harbors significant (unwelcome) doubts about them, is likely to have a difficult time being at all open-minded about these beliefs – let alone being open-minded in the deeper or truly Christian sense. Instead, she is likely to be anxious, irritable, defensive, and arrogant in the face of challenges to her beliefs. Likewise, a person whose grasp of his Christian beliefs is firm and well-informed may, while perhaps possessing the confidence and courage to be open-minded, nonetheless be *uninclined* to do so, for he might lack the kind of concern or love for his neighbor that would lead him to give a respectful, open-minded hearing to his neighbor's beliefs. On one plausible account, the richest source of such love is an intimate, experiential relationship with the One who *is* love.[19]

Baehr captures both dimensions of the rule of prayer: it grounds us in God and turns us toward authors in love. According to the rule of

prayer, we read aware of our deep nearness to God while actively pursuing nearness to God. The rule of prayer ensures that our empathetic encounter with an author's projected world is *fueled* and *sourced* by intimate connection to God in Christ.

Is there a disposition needed for the application of these rules? Yes, diligence. Too easily and too often we passively accept or reject an author's projected world based only on our initial impression or assumptions about the author – positive or negative. We must be diligent. When applied in community, these rules are wisdom for reading theology discerningly.

Wisdom 2: Forming the Virtues for Reading Theology

Are rules *all* we need? I don't believe so. There is more to reading theology wisely as a practice of the Christian faith, and the bulk of Christian wisdom before me would agree. We need more than rules – we need to become the kinds of readers who can apply these rules according to the pattern of Jesus Christ. We need the *virtues* appropriate for reading theology as disciples.[20]

Notice something about Chris's image. *You* stand with the author. You, with all of your history, faith traditions, hopes, and fears. You are there. You, dear reader, are part of the world in front of the reading you are seeking to inhabit. New ways of understanding yourself are possible here, and new ways of understanding others and God.[21]

Some of what you see in a work of theology will converge with your way of seeing the world, and some of it will diverge. Some of it will feel like home: familiar, safe, comforting, and confirming who you are. But other aspects of the author's projected world may feel foreign; some of it may even feel off base or dangerous. It may not be dangerous, but it may feel that way because of its foreignness to you. People who are different from us see the world differently than we do. Encountering such differences when reading theology may cause us to feel unsettled, unnerved, or even frightened. All of these responses make it difficult for us to "walk across the room" and see with the author.

To cross the room, we need more than tips and tricks, or rules. We also need more than a determined will. Wise teachers have long recognized that acting wisely involves more than willpower alone. We need to become *certain kinds of persons*, which is a way of saying that we need the *virtues* that are appropriate for reading theology as disciples.

A virtue is a *settled state of character*, and there are three that will help us see as the author sees. Talking about virtue is a way of getting at the settled dispositions which help us to act rightly, to do the right thing as a matter of course, almost like second nature. We might call these conditions of the heart, echoing back to Jesus's metaphor of fruit-bearing trees: "Make a tree good and its fruit will be good, or make a tree bad and its fruit will be bad, for a tree is recognized by its fruit. . . . For the mouth speaks what the heart is full of. A good man brings good things out of the good stored up in him, and an evil man brings evil things out of the evil stored up in him" (Matt. 12:33, 35). In keeping with the condition of one's heart, actions spring out. The virtues I am talking about follow the same principle. As the Holy Spirit works through our efforts at obedience to the way of Jesus, these three dispositions are formed in us over time: *receptivity*, *hospitality*, and *empathy*.

Can such dispositions be formed all at once? No, that has not been my experience, nor is it the collective wisdom of others. The formation of virtue requires time and intention (which recent scientific studies are bearing out).[22] Yet, I have found that students who practice these dispositions with intention find themselves surprised. As they read theology, they more readily find themselves standing at the author's shoulder, seeing her projected world.

The Virtue of Receptivity

Receptivity is the disposition of facing the author as a human being. I turn my shoulders toward her so she can address me face to face. If I can't face her as a person, then I'll never cross the room to see her projected world and consider whether it's a world I can live in.

Receptivity is grounded in the Christian imagination for reading presented in this book. Remember our work earlier: reading theology involves a living encounter with an author's world of meaning, *as a fellow member of Christ's body who is being conformed to Christ's image.* The author of whatever theological text we read is not only a person made in the image of God but also our sibling in Christ.

We are common members of the body of Christ. The author is a potential means through which the Holy Spirit may teach us, draw us closer into fellowship with Christ, and conform us to Christ's image. When we read theology as a means of sanctification, then receptivity toward brothers and sisters in Christ is simply *Christ-like.* To be clear, reading receptively doesn't necessarily mean I choose to live in the author's projected world. I may push back from it, but when the disposition of receptivity is formed in me, I'm able to cross the room to see as the author sees.

There is *hopefulness* in receptivity. As Christians, we look toward Christ in all things, hopeful that he is at work and that finally he will be the fulfillment of all our longings. But even in *this life*, we look *hopefully* – even expectantly – for signs of the in-breaking kingdom of God. That same hopefulness leads us to read theology receptively, waiting for God to meet us there.

The Virtue of Hospitality

Hospitality builds on receptivity. If I'm not being formed in receptivity – practicing it with intention, all the while receptive of the Spirit's activity – then hospitality will be a sham. In advance I will have decided what I think of this author's world of meaning. Before seeing as she sees, my mind is made up. That's not hospitality. Hospitality is two-sided. It entails *interchange* and *interaction*. The twentieth-century priest and writer Henri Nouwen expresses this as well as anyone I know:

> When hostility is converted into hospitality then fearful strangers can become guests revealing to their hosts the promise they are carrying with them. Then, in fact, the distinction between host and guest proves to be artificial and evaporates in the recognition of the new found unity. . . . Hospitality, therefore, means primarily the creation of a free space where the stranger can enter and become a friend instead of an enemy.[23]

A hospitable reader *receives* what the author offers, while *offering* interest and questions.

There is a wonderful African tradition known as the gift of the kola nut. Unlike in the West, where we bring a gift to our host, this tradition turns it around: the gift is given to the guest. In a beautiful African liturgical prayer, the kola nut symbolizes willingness to receive from Christ our guest. The prayer captures Jesus's *strange form of hospitality*. Sometimes Jesus is the host, and sometimes he's the guest. At the well with the Samaritan woman, Jesus plays the guest. He receives her hospitality, taking the water she offers. Then the dynamic shifts as he teaches her. He becomes her host, inviting her to a fresh way of seeing herself and God. With Zacchaeus, Jesus begins as guest then becomes the host. At the Pharisee's home, likewise, Jesus is the guest-turned-host. The African prayer mirrors Jesus's mysterious habit of guesting and hosting: "Christ our guest, we offer you kola-nut, a sign of friendship, fellowship, and welcome from our family. Accept it, and make our community your home. Christ our guest, share our joys and our sorrows which we present before you."[24] The kola nut is a sign of *mutuality* and *exchange*. The community prays that Jesus will accept their invitation to be with them and among them.

Can we, following the pattern of Jesus, read as both *guest* and *host*?

Let's not kid ourselves: intellectual hospitality is not a virtue in all quarters. For those who perceive knowledge in terms of possession and ownership, reading is the process by which content is conquered. For them, losing control is a driving fear, and thus consenting to be a guest makes little sense. Armed robbery or a castle siege are better descriptions of reading than guesting and hosting.

However, the account of reading I offer you invites an alternative vision, one not based on domination. When I begin as one who seeks to *love* the author as my brother or sister in Christ, then I seek as a matter of course to embody a posture of receptivity toward them, receiving what they offer as I assume the role of guest. Reading thus shifts from mastery to *intimacy*.

When reading shifts in this way, we understand that, as theologian Paul Griffiths explains, "objects of knowledge . . . can be loved and contemplated, but they cannot be dominated by sequestration."[25] He means that knowledge cannot be taken for myself as a possession, hoarded, or cordoned off. I'm never the ultimate possessor of knowledge. That right is God's alone. We know things as they participate in God, but only God's knowledge of them is total and exhaustive.[26] Our creaturely knowledge is only ever a small participation in the vast, unending knowledge that is God's alone *as God*. Whatever I know, and whatever I grow to know through reading, is only ever a gift to me from God, mediated to me through a human author.

The virtue of hospitality enables us to read as both *guests* and *hosts*. We offer our attention and goodwill. We receive what the author gives, expecting intimacy rather than mastery.

The Virtue of Empathy

Receptivity enables hospitality. Hospitality promotes empathy. Each moves us closer to the author's projected world, until we stand at her shoulder. And with proximity comes *risk*.

Receptivity requires attention, and such attention makes me vulnerable to the author. By facing her, I expose my own face. "Attention is the rarest and purest form of generosity," as twentieth-century philosopher Simone Weil says.[27] Facing another person is generous. I don't glance over my shoulder at them or guard myself by running past. I slow down, stop, and face them as a person made in the image of God. Even as I expose my face, I'm able to receive.

Hospitality is a more intimate proximity. Having faced the author, I now consider her, listen to her, and inquire of her. I become her *guest*; hospitality invites mutual exchange. Writer and educator David Smith writes that "Good questions communicate the willingness to not know and to learn from the other. Sincere questions imply that I really want to hear the answer, and am not just looking for ways to display my own knowledge."[28] Honest questions are a trustworthy sign of hospitable reading. We find ourselves asking, "How is it that the author can see the world this way? What do I notice from this vantage point that I don't notice from my own vantage point? What would it require of me to live in this world? Am I willing to do that?" Feels risky, right? The author's gifts may change me in unexpected ways, and I may even push back from the world they project.

It's no wonder that empathy is the hardest and riskiest virtue of all three. It requires that I think and feel *with* the author, that I seek to stand *with* her. Psychologist Jamil Zaki has been researching empathy for years, and he explains that it includes three ways of responding to one another: emotional empathy, motivational empathy, and cognitive empathy.[29] Cognitive empathy is the kind required of wise theology readers: "explicitly considering someone else's perspective."[30] We will probably find this challenging, but we shouldn't despair. Zaki's studies show that people who work at empathy find that it grows and expands like a muscle. His studies also suggest that empathy's three facets are intertwined, so we shouldn't be surprised if cognitive empathy carries over into our emotions and volition: "Sharing someone else's emotion draws our attention to what they feel, and thinking with them reliably increases our concern for their well-being."[31] Thus, when adopting an author's vantage point — standing at her shoulder, seeing as she sees — we may find ourselves *caring* about her.

Wisdom 3: Discerning the Risks of Empathy

Reading theology as inhabitation is about proximity; it moves us *close* to theology – so close that we see the world as the author sees it. The receptive, hospitable, empathetic proximity I'm describing is more than mere exposure. More than merely observing her world, I struggle across the room to see it *as* she sees it. As C. S. Lewis wrote, I seek "to imagine with other imaginations, to feel with other hearts, as well as with [my] own."[32] Such proximity makes me vulnerable. I risk being the guest of the author, admitting my needs, and receiving the gifts she wishes to offer. Her gifts may reveal what I wish to conceal. Her gifts may uncover my ignorance or naiveté, or, more painfully, my willful commitment to falsehood. Her gifts might also reveal insecurities or fear, which is very common when studying theology. Fear arises when theology puts my idols at risk or deconstructs my tidy God-boxes.

In short, empathetic proximity puts me at risk of *change*. In the best cases, inhabiting a theological space changes me for the better as my knowledge of God aligns more truly with God's knowledge of himself and my life aligns more truly with the truth of myself in Christ. In the worst cases, I encounter a theological space that projects a false and hateful world.

We may so enjoy the sense of comradery and humanity of empathetic reading that we fail to consider the influence and sway that such a world may have over us. Standing at her shoulder, we may not consider the question, Is it the real world? The emotional power of empathy leads psychologist Paul Bloom to argue that empathy actually harms our ability to act justly and compassionately. We feel with another person so strongly that our capacity for *rational compassion* is diminished.[33] Reading theology empathetically requires wisdom so that we can inhabit the author's world while not diminishing our capacity for discerning the truth of the projected worlds we encounter.

Consider the case of the award-winning actor Ben Kingsley, who portrayed Adolf Eichmann in the film *Operation Finale* (2018). Eichmann was the infamous Nazi ideologue behind Hitler's plan to exterminate the Jews. Kingsley is Jewish, and portraying Eichmann empathetically could place Kingsley's sense of self at risk. So, when an interviewer asked Kingsley about "getting inside the mind" of Eichmann, he said,

> I didn't – that was the secret. Let's imagine I'm a portrait artist. This man was in my studio, I had him in one corner, I had my canvas in front of me, and I put him directly onto the canvas. I was not a conduit for him. His ideology was not the guiding force for my performance. The guiding force for my performance was the victims, and his silhouette was molded by their accusation, by their memory, by their reverberating grief – but nothing from that man ever touched me or entered me. I simply transferred his image onto canvas, by that I mean film. He never got close to me, he never got near me, he never infected me.[34]

He refused to get near Eichmann on account of what nearness could do to him. He refused empathy because of its risk. Empathy would place Kingsley closer to Eichmann than he was willing to go.

Kingsley wisely understood that portraying Eichmann empathetically would be a kind of inhabitation in Eichmann's world. His refusal to do so reminds us that the empathy required for real inhabitation puts us at risk. We get close enough to the author – indeed we stand at her shoulder – that we see *with her*. When the world is true, we live more truly into the truth of God, and when the world is false, then empathy puts us in harm's way.

In the case of Kingsley, however, his acting craft allows him to engage without risk – but also without empathy. Many readers of theology don't realize that a projected world stands before them. We are savvy enough about television shows and movies to know they project more than facts and assertions, but we stumble with that basic fact when it comes to works of theology. Do works of theology include facts and assertions? Definitely; those are part and parcel of the world *of* such works. Comprehending them is essential to us if we wish to discern what the work is *about*: a possible way of seeing the world in light of

God. What architect Juhani Pallasmaa says of architecture is equally true for theology: "Architecture frames, structures, re-orients, scales, refocuses and slows down our experience of the world and makes it an ingredient of the embodied sense of our own being; it always has a mediating role instead of being the end itself."[35] A work of theology organizes behavior because it projects a world the author believes is the *true world*. "This is God and the world as they *actually are*." What if the author is wrong? What if the world she projects, the world we encounter as empathetic readers, is *not the world as it really is*?

Like Kingsley, C. S. Lewis understood the risks of empathy. Reading *is* empathy for Lewis: "to imagine with other imaginations, to feel with other hearts, as well as with our own."[36] But he also knew its costs firsthand.

Lewis describes the cost of empathy when writing the character Screwtape in his best-selling book *The Screwtape Letters*. Screwtape is a demon who corresponds with his nephew Wormwood, a young demon-in-training, about his experiences tempting and tormenting a Christian. Writing the dialogue required Lewis to empathize with the demon, thinking demonic thoughts. In a sense, Lewis had to live *within* the projected world that would be the true world for a demon. It affected Lewis so profoundly that he refused ever to write another word in the voice of Screwtape.

> Though I had never written anything more easily, I never wrote with less enjoyment. The ease came, no doubt, from the fact that the device of diabolical letters, once you have thought of it, exploits itself spontaneously. . . . It would run away with you for a thousand pages if you gave it its head. But though it was easy to twist one's mind into the diabolical attitude, it was not fun, or not for long. The strain produced a sort of spiritual cramp. The work into which I had to project myself while I spoke through Screwtape was all dust, grit, thirst, and itch. Every trace of beauty, freshness, and geniality had to be excluded. It almost smothered me before I was done. It would have smothered my readers if I had prolonged it.[37]

Lewis understood the risk of empathy because he experienced it firsthand. Applied to a corrupting influence, it almost smothered him.

Inhabiting theology puts the reader at risk, not of suffocation necessarily, but of being so close to the reading that the encounter changes you. Maybe for the better. Maybe not. Most often, I believe, reading theology changes us for the better. It aligns our knowledge of God more and more with God's own knowledge of himself. We find ourselves drawn toward our true selves as the Spirit works in the world of meaning created by our siblings in Christ who wrote the theology we read.

We must not forget that *persons* build the theological spaces we inhabit. Persons with incomplete and distorted grasps of things, like us. Persons on the way to holiness, like us. Sometimes the world projected for us is *incomplete* because the author was ignorant or misinformed. Other projected worlds are *distortions* founded on overreactions to the challenges of the author's setting, or they are founded on willful exclusions of relevant information or perspectives. No work of theology is complete or perfect. We should no more expect perfection of theological works than we expect perfection from our dearest friends and family. The risks of empathy are thus acute but not unusual. To summarize, the worlds projected for us in theological works are incomplete and potentially distorted, and reading empathetically risks embracing those incomplete and distorted worlds.

However (and this is a very big however), refusing to read empathetically is *itself* a risk. It risks fashioning a world full of excluded strangers and limiting ourselves to an increasingly small world under the illusion of our control. Let me explain.

First, the refusal to read empathetically risks a world full of excluded strangers. As Christians, we are siblings of one body, knit together by the Spirit of God. In the deepest and most significant way, then, we are *not* strangers to each other. Yes, when reading theology, we may find each other surprisingly *strange*, but the strangeness of an author is not necessarily her falsehood. We would never wish for others to assume this about us, would we? We would not wish for Christian siblings to encounter our strangeness, assume we are false, and exclude us, right? Refusing to read empathetically risks fashioning a world full of excluded strangers, siblings in Christ kept at bay because of their difference.

Second, refusing empathy risks limiting ourselves to an increasingly small world under the illusion of our control. We should not pretend that every projected world is one we wish to inhabit. We will see as some authors see and say to them, "No thank you." And to others even, "No, even though you are my sibling in Christ, *this* is not the world of the Living God!" However, stepping away from the threshold of an author's world is not a wholly negative experience. Though uncomfortable, it enlarges our world and reveals our desire for control. As Rowan Williams explains, "Recognizing the other as other without the immediate impulse to make them the same involves recognizing the incompleteness of the world I think I can manage and moving into the world which I may not be able to manage so well, but which has more depth of reality. And that must be to move closer to God."[38]

We sometimes, maybe often, push away from strangers because their difference, their otherness, unsettles us. That unsettling is precisely what we desperately *need.* The experience opens us to perceive our incomplete grasp on things. The world is not as tidy as we think, and our impulse to use theology for control and manipulation, for structuring a world very much in our grasp, is great among us all. Such a world is not the real world. Moving away from a small world under the illusion of our control only moves us closer to God. Only God's view of the world is total. Only God's grasp of things is complete.

Confronting the stranger *as stranger* brings us back to our first kind of wisdom: reading by the rules. How do we let her enlarge our world while also determining whether we can live in her world? Shall we cross the threshold? How shall we know when to leap into the projected world of one theology but push back from the world of another? We must read empathetically and *wisely*.

Prayer

Wise God,
We are full of many things that hide what we lack:

Full of ourselves – without humility to confess God.
Full of food – without temperance to stop eating.
Full of promises – without diligence to follow through.
Full of entertainment – without love for truth, goodness,
and beauty.
Full of freedoms – without generosity to extend them to all.
Full of power – without courage to pursue peace.
Full of knowledge – without faith to rest in God.
Full of theology to read – without wisdom.
As we read theology, wise God,
instruct us and form us
that we would read wisely as part of our Christian life –
more like Jesus every day,
more truly ourselves, and
more committed to loving our neighbors.

Summary

In the world *of* theology, we discover the author's projected world and possible way of living. There we engage what the author says and what her work as a whole is about. In the world *in front* of theology, however, the reader as an embodied human person engages that world. While the worlds *behind* and *of* the page don't change, the world *in front* changes with every new reader. You, the reader, comprise the particular world in front of the theology you read. The big question is, Will you *live* according to this world? Three wisdoms are required to answer this question well: (1) the wisdom to read by the rules – the rule of Scripture, the rule of faith, the rule of love, and the rule of prayer; (2) the wisdom to form the appropriate virtues – receptivity, hospitality, and empathy; and (3) the wisdom to discern the risks of empathy.

Questions for Reflection and Discussion

1. What are the features of your *world in front* that most influence how you read theology?

2. How would you hold the four rules together as you read theology (wisdom 1)?
3. If you sought to intentionally cultivate the three virtues of wise reading (wisdom 2), what would that look like in your life?

Theology Lab: Compose Your Credo

I have been crucified with Christ and I no longer live . . .

— *Galatians* 2:20

Credo (n; Lat.): an idea or set of beliefs that guides the actions of a person or group.

Theologians don't only listen — patiently, responsively, diligently — they also speak. Indeed, they must. Unless we know how, as Karl Barth put it, to "walk warily around the burning bush," the practice of theology puts us at risk, for it demands that we say something of God.[39]

Your credo expresses your belief in God. The essentials. You believe many things about God, but your credo states that which is most essential, nonnegotiable. The following metaphors are helpful:

Your credo is your *foundation* upon which your beliefs about everything else is built, from which you live your life, and on which your hopes are founded.

Your credo is the *center of the orbit* around which everything else that you believe revolves, some beliefs closer to the center than others, but the center remains.

Your credo is the *epicenter of the web* of your beliefs. The center of the web has many threads running out from it and provides each thread with a sure anchor; pull on any one thread and it leads you back to the center.

Part 1: What Do You Believe?

Compose and explain your credo in six hundred words. Summarize in your own words the most basic and central elements that are included when you say, "I believe in God." This is your credo.

Part 2: Why Do You Believe What You Believe?

Try to identify the sources from which you draw in identifying what you believe. Your sources will include at least (1) Scripture, (2) experience (your life, your family), and (3) tradition (the Christian tradition passed down through the generations, or your church tradition).

Part 3: What Difference Does It Make?

How do these beliefs direct your life? Said differently: How is your walking about – your movements throughout the day as you put one foot in front of the other – affected, shaped, directed by these beliefs?

Part 4: Proclaim It

After having written your credo, verbalize it to three people, then invite their questions. What you share should focus on the content of your credo, but it should also include some mention of your rationale for believing (sources), and how your credo compels you to live ("direction"). Be sure to include at least one concrete way it leads you to worship (doxology) and live (direction).

Sending

"Come and see," said Philip.

—John 1:46

A writer of theology, like Philip,
has seen something of God and wishes to show you.
Read what she offers as a sibling in Christ.
Pray often, and pray like you mean it.
Love the author as your neighbor.
Be ready for surprises.
Grow in wisdom.
Be at peace.

Acknowledgments

I NEED TO THANK MANY PEOPLE for their companionship.

James and the team at Eerdmans believed in the work and got it between covers. Austin, Logan, Emily, and Holly: Thank you for helping me, over all those cups of coffee, to find the right voice and tone for this book. Chris Koelle: How can I begin thanking you for collaborating over these years of writing and for your amazing art? No words suffice (but I trust that you know, Chris). Suzanne, Kyle, Fred, Laurie, Mike, Dan, and David: Thank you for helping me see this work through your students' eyes. Breanna, Emilee, Nick, Mark, Katlyn, Sawyer, Ben, Megan, Hannah, Arie, Zakry, Theresa, John, Matt, Eustace, Laura, and Mom: Thank you for hanging around after class, joining me for lunch, or sharing a cup of coffee to discuss bits from this book — your insightful, honest, and wise feedback helped me immensely! Bo Helmich, my dear friend, thank you for the Fellowship of Theologians. Your generosity and theological wisdom astound me. Tammy, Hannah, Abby, and Samuel: You are . . . what can I say? You are my heart. Thank you for loving me and for supporting my calling.

I am also grateful for the generous sabbatical leave provided by Huntington University, and for the university donors who funded my collaboration with Chris Koelle (and, of course, for Vince, who cast such a compelling vision to them). Finally, though it may sound corny, I mean it sincerely: I'm thankful to the great cloud of Christian witnesses upon whose shoulders I stood as I composed this book. Having introduced you to a few of them, I hope that you will go and read them wisely!

Appendix

Caravaggio, *The Incredulity of St. Thomas* (1601–1602)

Lucas Cranach the Younger, Weimar Altarpiece (1555)

Raoul Dufy, *Interior with Open Windows* (1928)

Notes

Chapter 1

1. Louis I. Kahn, *Louis I. Kahn: Writings, Lectures, Interviews*, ed. Alessandra Latour (New York: Rizzoli, 1991), 75.

2. This usage is consistent with the views of others who have spoken about human perception in the last hundred years. I am thinking of Gaston Bachelard, Maurice Merleau-Ponty, Pierre Bourdieu, Michel de Certeau, Michael Polanyi, Étienne Wenger, and Charles Taylor. I have written elsewhere about the relation between imagination and theology: Kent Eilers, "Embodying Faithfulness: New Monastic Retrieval and the Christian Imagination," in *Marking the Church: Essays in Ecclesiology*, ed. Gregory Scott Peters and Matt Jenson (Eugene, OR: Wipf & Stock, 2016), 92–110; Kent Eilers, "Jonathan Edwards and Wolfhart Pannenberg toward Trinitarian Prayer," in *The Ecumenical Edwards*, ed. Kyle Strobel (Surrey: Ashgate, 2015), 213–33.

3. David I. Smith and Susan M. Felch, *Teaching and Christian Imagination* (Grand Rapids: Eerdmans, 2016), 3.

4. It is a moment of "fusing horizons," as Hans-Georg Gadamer would phrase it. The author's "horizon" of meaning overlaps with the horizon of meaning experienced by any Christian suffering persecution, regardless of the time and place. See Hans-Georg Gadamer, *Truth and Method* (New York: Continuum, 2004).

5. I am following the translation of John H. Elliot, *1 Peter: A New Translation with Introduction and Commentary* (New York: Doubleday, 2001).

6. Étienne Wenger, *Communities of Practice: Learning, Meaning, and Identity* (Cambridge: Cambridge University Press, 1998), 176.

7. I'm aware that, by offering a distinctly theological imagination for reading, my approach contrasts with that of Paul Griffiths in *Religious Reading: The Place of Reading in the Practice of Religion* (Oxford: Oxford University Press, 1999), 4–6.

8. I depart from literary theorist Paul Ricoeur's view at this point, granting the author a greater degree of agency in determining what the reader apprehends of a written text's meaning. Ricoeur argues that texts are autonomous once written,

but I disagree. The author's agency is still extended to the reader through the text, and this is the case whether the reader interprets the text according to the author's initial intentions or not. For further development of these arguments, see Kevin J. Vanhoozer, *Is There a Meaning in This Text? The Bible, the Reader, and the Morality of Literary Knowledge* (Grand Rapids: Zondervan, 1980), 107–10; Nicholas Wolterstorff, *Divine Discourse: Philosophical Reflections on the Claim That God Speaks* (Cambridge: Cambridge University Press, 1995).

9. Paul Ricoeur, *Interpretation Theory: Discourse and the Surplus of Meaning* (Fort Worth: Texas Christian University Press, 1976), 37, 88.

10. Roy Anker, *Catching Light: Looking for God in the Movies* (Grand Rapids: Eerdmans, 2004), 4.

11. Marilynne Robinson, *The Givenness of Things: Essays* (New York: Picador, 2015), 15. Emphasis added.

12. Ricoeur, *Interpretation Theory*, 87.

13. Karl Barth makes a similar comparison when forming relations between the Word of God *as Jesus*, the Word of God *as Scripture*, and the Word of God *as the preacher's proclamation*. See Karl Barth, *The Göttingen Dogmatics: Instruction in the Christian Religion*, ed. Hannelotte Reiffen, trans. Geoffrey W. Bromiley (Grand Rapids: Eerdmans, 1991), 1:14–41.

14. Murali Balaji, "The Theology of White Nationalism, the Inevitability of Charlottesville, and the Imagined America," *Huffington Post*, August 17, 2017, https://www.huffpost.com/entry/the-theology-of-white-nationalism-the-inevitability_b_5995dac1e4b02eb2fda31df3.

15. Aelred of Rievaulx, *Spiritual Friendship: The Classic Text with a Spiritual Commentary by Dennis Billy*, trans. M. Eugenia Laker (Notre Dame: Ave Maria, 2008), 61.

16. See Alan Jacobs, *A Theology of Reading: The Hermeneutics of Love* (Boulder, CO: Westview, 2001).

17. Helmut Thielicke, *A Little Exercise for Young Theologians* (Grand Rapids: Eerdmans, 1962), 34.

18. Thielicke, *Little Exercise*, 34. Emphasis added.

19. James H. Cone, *The Cross and the Lynching Tree* (Maryknoll, NY: Orbis, 2011), 166.

20. Miguel A. De La Torre, *Burying White Privilege: Resurrecting a Badass Christianity* (Grand Rapids: Eerdmans, 2018), 25–26.

21. See the final remarks in chapter 4 and the four rules for reading theology in chapter 7 that all apply when reading heresy.

22. Karl Barth, *Evangelical Theology: An Introduction* (Grand Rapids: Eerdmans, 1963), 64.

23. St. Francis of Assisi, "A Letter to Brother Anthony of Padua," in *Francis of Assisi: Early Documents*, ed. Regis J. Armstrong, J. A. Wayne Hellmann, and William J. Short (New York: New City Press, 1999), 1:107.

24. Timothy Gallagher, *The Examen Prayer: Ignatian Wisdom for Our Lives Today* (New York: Crossroad, 2006), 36. Ignatius outlines his practice of the examen in his *Spiritual Exercises*, No. 43. The phrase "rummaging for God" is borrowed from Dennis Hamm, SJ, "Rummaging for God: Praying Backwards through Your Day," *America*, May 14, 1994, http://www.ignatianspirituality.com/ignatian-prayer/the-examen/rummaging-for-god-praying-backward-through-your-day/.

Chapter 2

1. Juhani Pallasmaa, *The Eyes of the Skin: Architecture and the Senses*, 3rd ed. (London: John Wiley & Sons, 2012), 76.

2. Here I focus primarily on theology as a practice and process, but the word "theology" also names the knowledge of God that we gain through the process. In this sense, theology is craft *and* content; process *and* possession. This is a very ancient observation. Early Christian theologians often called the knowledge of God – that knowledge which is unlike every other kind of knowledge in fundamental and significant ways because it concerns the Living, triune God – simply *theologia*.

3. Evagrius Ponticus, *Chapters on Prayer*, in *The Philokalia: The Complete Text; Compiled by St. Nikodimos of the Holy Mountain and St. Makarios of Corinth*, ed. and trans. G. E. H. Palmer, Philip Sherrard, and Kallistos Ware, rev. ed. (New York: Farrar, Straus and Giroux, 1983), 1.61.

4. You may become aware, as you spend time around folks who study and discuss theology, that some believe theology's object is not God himself but the language of the believing community, or their practices and beliefs. Others are less confident that theology can even claim that level of directness, so they make the human *experience* of God the object of theology. Let me suggest, instead, that theology's proper object is the Living God. As such, theology's object is extraordinarily different from anything else that receives our attention. The importance of this distinction should be increasingly apparent in what follows.

5. Karl Barth, *Evangelical Theology: An Introduction* (Grand Rapids: Eerdmans, 1963), 7.

6. C. S. Lewis, *Prince Caspian* (New York: HarperCollins, 2001), 380.

7. A. W. Tozer, *The Knowledge of the Holy* (New York: HarperCollins, 1961), 6.

8. Two millennia of Christian thinking about the nature of God's "grace" stands behind that sentence, which I cannot unpack here. See Kent Eilers, "The

Grammar of Grace," Forrester Lecture Series, Huntington University (April 21, 2021), https://www.youtube.com/watch?v=nA2PE05NGyo; Kent Eilers, "Introduction," in *The Grammar of Grace: Readings from the Christian Tradition*, ed. Kent Eilers, Ashley Cocksworth, and Anna Silvas (Eugene, OR: Cascade, 2019), xxvii–xxxix; John M. G. Barclay, *Paul and the Power of Grace* (Grand Rapids: Eerdmans, 2019); John M. G. Barclay, *Paul and the Gift* (Grand Rapids: Eerdmans, 2015).

9. Mark McIntosh, *Divine Teaching: An Introduction to Christian Theology* (Hoboken, NJ: Wiley-Blackwell, 2007), 3.

10. "Self-enclosed worlds" is the phrase used by Miroslav Volf and Maurice Lee in "The Spirit and the Church," in *Advents of the Spirit: An Introduction to the Current Study of Pneumatology*, ed. Bradford E. Hinze and D. Lyle Dabney (Milwaukee: Marquette University Press, 2001), 394.

11. John Calvin, *Institutes of the Christian Religion*, trans. Henry Beveridge (Grand Rapids: Eerdmans, 1989), 37.

12. Catherine of Siena, *The Dialogue*, trans. Suzanne Noffke, OP (Mahwah, NJ: Paulist, 1980), 48.

13. "Mystery" is a term often thrown around unthoughtfully in theology. Let me explain what I mean by it. Theological mystery entails all that transcends our comprehension as it concerns God. Even as we know God really and truly, vast reaches of God's life remain that our theology will never fully plumb. That is theological mystery. Imagine a person living in a two-dimensional world confronted with a three-dimensional object, like a cylinder. The cylinder stands before her, but a circle is all the 2-D person grasps of it. Even as she sees the circle truly, more of the cylinder always remains. This is what Steven Boyer and Christopher Hall term the "dimensional" sense of theological mystery. See Steven D. Boyer and Christopher A. Hall, *The Mystery of God: Theology for Knowing the Unknowable* (Grand Rapids: Baker Academic, 2012). To discover what this could mean for theological education, see Kent Eilers, "Encountering Mystery in the Classroom," *Didaktikos* 4, no. 1 (September 2020): 27–28. Last, it must be said: accepting the presence of mystery in theology is essential. Without it, your theology quietly and disastrously slips into study not actually concerned with the Living God. Whatever you think you capture within your tight theological grip, it's not God. St. Augustine gestures in this direction in a couple sermons: "If you understand, it isn't God" (Sermon 117); "For if you have fully grasped what you want to say, it isn't God. If you have been able to comprehend it, you have comprehended something else instead of God. If you think you have been able to comprehend, your thoughts have deceived you" (Sermon 52). (Both sermons translated by E. Hill, *The Works of Saint Augustine: A Translation for the 21st Century* [New York: New City Press, 1991 and 1992 respectively], Sermons, III/3, 209–23; III/4, 50–65). Many nuances present

themselves to the reader with these remarks, which are capably navigated in Jean Grondin, "Augustine's 'Si comprehendis, non est Deus': To What Extent Is God Incomprehensible?," *Analecta Hermeneutica* 9 (2017): 1–13.

14. Anselm of Canterbury, *Proslogion*, in *Proslogium; Monologium; An Appendix in behalf of the Fool by Gaunilon; and "Cur Deus Homo,"* trans. Sidney Norton Deane (Chicago: Open Court, 1926), 2. Augustine says nearly the same in Sermon 43, trans. R. G. MacMullen, in *St. Augustin: "Sermon on the Mount," "Harmony of the Gospels," "Homilies on the Gospels,"* in vol. 6 of *Nicene and Post-Nicene Fathers of the Christian Church*, ed. Philip Schaff (Buffalo, NY: Christian Literature Co., 1888), par. 7, 9.

15. I'm grateful to Bo Helmich for helping me see this in St. Anselm. The whole person was also the concern for Jesus. Jesus was never merely after the mind. The Gospels often reference sight, as both visual faculty and metaphor, to express this connection. Repeatedly, they show that merely looking at Jesus wasn't sufficient to understand him, to *see* him. Catching sight of Jesus only led to true understanding when that sight involved the turning of one's heart and allegiance toward him in confession and obedience. Such turning signaled authentic perception rather than mere looking. See Ola Sigurdson, *Heavenly Bodies: Incarnation, the Gaze, and Embodiment in Christian Theology* (Grand Rapids: Eerdmans, 2016), chap. 5.

16. Walter Brueggemann, *Awed to Heaven, Rooted to Earth: Prayers of Walter Brueggemann* (Minneapolis: Fortress, 2002), 3.

17. Thomas Aquinas, *The Summa Theologica of St. Thomas Aquinas*, trans. Fathers of the English Dominican Province, rev. ed. (London: Burns, Oates, & Washbourne, 1920), I.1.7.

18. I like how Sam Wells and Abby Kocher explain it: "Those leading intercessions – speaking back to God the people's need in the light of God's story – are . . . placing our own lyric suffering and apprehension in the light of the epic landscape of God's providence; and they are setting the lyric plight of peoples near and far in the context of an epic sense of the well-being of the world – even the universe – as a whole. It is this interplay of intense, personal, urgent need and larger, broader civilization and providence that makes prayers so hard to prepare but so vital to the congregation's sense of its place in the world and in God's purposes." Samuel Wells and Abigail Kocher, *Shaping the Prayers of the People: The Art of Intercession* (Grand Rapids: Eerdmans, 2014), 12.

19. Anselm, *Proslogion* 2; Augustine, Sermon 43, par. 7, 9.

20. John Webster, *God without Measure: Working Papers in Christian Theology*, vol. 1 (London: T&T Clark, 2015), 3.

21. See William C. Placher, *The Domestication of Transcendence: How Modern Thinking about God Went Wrong* (Louisville: Westminster John Knox, 1996).

22. Kate Sonderegger says this profoundly: "We have creaturely words, creaturely intellect and ability, that have been given and possess a likeness that breaks through to its Giver, and enters that Hiddenness with words that negate, that deny, and in their own key, affirm temporal things as signs for Things Eternal" (*Systematic Theology*, vol. 1 [Minneapolis: Fortress, 2015], 105–6). Kate remains confident, as I do, that God condescends to us in such a way that the knowledge of God may be expressed through our language (the "likeness" she speaks of). Yet, at the same time, this likeness cannot be taken to mean that our words exhaust who God is or what God does. A "hiddenness" remains. Kate taps into one of the longest-standing tensions inherent in Christian theology.

23. Ephrem the Syrian, "On Human Language about God" (*Of Faith* 31), in *Ephrem the Syrian: Select Poems*, trans. Sebastian P. Brock and George A. Kiraz (Provo, UT: Brigham Young University Press, 2006), 19.

24. St. Gregory the Great, *Morals on the Book of Job*, trans. Members of the English Church (Oxford: John Henry Parker, 1844), vol. 1, epistle, part 4. Augustine of Hippo says, "How wonderful are your Scriptures! How profound! We see their surface and it attracts us like children. And yet, O my God, their depth is stupendous. We shudder to peer deep into them, for they inspire in us both the awe of reverence and the thrill of love" (*Confessions*, trans. R. S. Pine-Coffin (New York: Penguin Classics), 442–43 (book 12, part 14).

25. There are various ways to say this. Some would say theology concerns everything because everything "participates" in God. Others would say theology concerns everything because everything is "upheld" or sustained by God. The first speaks of a deep metaphysical relation all things share with God's very being, and the other speaks more of God's providential care and provision for all things. Behind these slight variations are different ways of conceiving the nature of the relation that God has to all things. I'm taking a middle path here that I hope resonates with both.

26. This is how Timothy George translates the Latin from the opening lines of Ames's *The Marrow of Sacred Divinity*: "Theologia est scientia vivendo Deo" (I.i.1). See George, foreword to *The Pastor Theologian: Resurrecting an Ancient Vision*, by Gerald Heistand and Todd Wilson (Grand Rapids: Zondervan, 2015), xv. The Latin can also be translated this way, but I like George's better: "Theology is the doctrine or teaching of living to God" (William Ames, *The Marrow of Theology*, trans. John Dykstra Eusden [Grand Rapids: Baker, 1997], 77). Karl Barth has the same instinct. He said you should "take your Bible and take your newspaper, and read both. But interpret newspapers from your Bible" (quoted in "Barth in Retirement," *Time*, May 31, 1963). Barth is saying that whatever is happening in your world, it relates to God and should be understood in the light of God's word.

27. See Perry L. Glanzer, Nathan F. Alleman, and Todd C. Ream, *Restoring the Soul of the University: Unifying Christian Higher Education in a Fragmented Age* (Downers Grove, IL: InterVarsity Press, 2017), 31–38. As they point out, letting theology sit in the queen's throne created unintended problems we should avoid. Rather than establishing theology as the foundation – the interpretive and guiding norm for all fields of study – theology moved apart from the other disciplines.

28. As McIntosh describes it, one can study theology as a "particular kind of instrument, an apt conceptuality, for exploring various dimensions of life" (McIntosh, *Divine Teaching*, 14).

29. Some call this the *prevenient grace* of God, and others use the term *common grace* to name it. The terms one uses depend on one's tradition of interpreting the relation between election and free will. Some will say that God's prevenient grace removes the barrier of sin from all people to make possible a grace-enabled response. Others will say that such prevenient grace moves only upon the elect. Common to both traditions, however, is the same theological commitment: grace must precede for us sinful humans to be reconciled to God.

30. Hans Urs von Balthasar, *Prayer*, trans. Graham Harrison (San Francisco: Ignatius, 1986), 76.

31. N. T. Wright, "The Prayer of the Trinity," http://ntwrightpage.com/2016/04/05/the-prayer-of-the-trinity/.

32. Modified from its responsive form: Faith Alive Christian Resources, *The Worship Sourcebook* (Grand Rapids: Baker, 2004), 719.

Chapter 3

1. Steen Eiler Rasmussen, *Experiencing Architecture* (Cambridge, MA: MIT Press, 1962), 33.

2. Paul J. Griffiths, *Intellectual Appetite: A Theological Grammar* (Washington, DC: Catholic University of America Press, 2009), 21.

3. Alan Jacobs, *A Theology of Reading: The Hermeneutics of Love* (Boulder, CO: Westview, 2001), 12.

4. Jacobs, *Theology of Reading*, 13.

5. You will find a more detailed account of what I say here just about anywhere in the writings of Paul Ricoeur, Hans-Georg Gadamer, or Kevin Vanhoozer, but I suggest looking as well to St. Augustine's *On Christian Teaching*, book 4.

6. Alain de Botton, *The Architecture of Happiness* (London: Hamish Hamilton, 2006), 71–72. Emphasis added to the final phrase.

7. Marilyn McEntyre, *Caring for Words in a Culture of Lies*, 2nd ed. (Grand Rapids: Eerdmans, 2021), 72, 78. Emphasis added.

8. Juhani Pallasmaa, *The Eyes of the Skin: Architecture and the Senses*, 3rd ed. (London: John Wiley & Sons, 2012), 48.

9. Ricoeur describes this process as following the "arrow" of the work: "To understand a text is to follow its movement from sense to reference: from what it says, to what it talks about. . . . Only the interpretation that complies with the injunction of the text, that follows the arrow of the sense and that tries to think accordingly, initiates a new self-understanding" (Ricoeur, *Interpretation Theory: Discourse and the Surplus of Meaning* [Fort Worth: Texas Christian University Press, 1976], 87, 94).

10. Ricoeur calls this the "sense" of a text. Ricoeur, *Interpretation Theory*, 87.

11. De Botton, *Architecture of Happiness*, 72.

12. Flannery O'Connor, *The Habit of Being: Letters of Flannery O'Connor*, ed. Sally Fitzgerald (New York: Farrar, Straus & Giroux, 1979), 458.

13. De Botton, *Architecture of Happiness*, 71–72.

14. Ricoeur, *Interpretation Theory*, 88.

15. Roy Anker, *Catching Light: Looking for God in the Movies* (Grand Rapids: Eerdmans, 2004), 5.

16. See the documents from the Synod of Hieria available at the Internet Medieval Source Book, https://sourcebooks.fordham.edu/source/icono-cncl754.asp.

17. St. John Damascene, *On Holy Images*, trans. Mary H. Allies (London: Thomas Baker, 1898; Internet Medieval Source Book, 1998), part 1, https://sourcebooks.fordham.edu/basis/johndamascus-images.asp.

18. This is a basic difference between Greek and Latin theology during the Patristic era that we could trace across a great many different sources. See Kent Eilers, Ashley Cocksworth, and Anna Silvas, eds., *The Grammar of Grace: Readings from the Christian Tradition* (Eugene, OR: Cascade, 2019), section 1.

19. See William Dyrness, *Visual Faith: Art, Theology, and Worship in Dialogue* (Grand Rapids: Baker Academic, 2001); Jim Forest, *Praying with Icons* (Maryknoll, NY: Orbis, 1997); Rowan Williams, *The Dwelling of the Light: Praying with the Icons of Christ* (Grand Rapids: Eerdmans, 2003).

20. Rowan Williams, *Christ on Trial: How the Gospel Unsettles Our Judgement* (Grand Rapids: Eerdmans, 2003), 50.

21. The twentieth-century philosopher Hans-Georg Gadamer would ask the question this way: how does the "horizon" of Luke's Gospel meet the "horizon" of the reader? He means that every act of interpretation happens from the perspective of one's own historical, cultural, and experiential setting. Those features of your life comprise your horizon. Just look up from the book for a moment and find the horizon. You see that particular horizon because of where you are sitting in the moment that you read this book. Gadamer takes that as a metaphor for interpretation to compel you to pay attention to your horizon *and* to pay attention to the

horizon of the text you're reading, which was comprised of the author's particular historical, cultural, and experiential setting. Interpretation, for Gadamer, entailed the "fusing of horizons" between text and reader. See Hans-Georg Gadamer, *Truth and Method* (New York: Continuum, 2004), especially 302–7, 576–77.

22. Joel B. Green, *The Gospel of Luke*, The New International Commentary on the New Testament (Grand Rapids: Eerdmans, 1997), 9.

23. Williams, *Christ on Trial*, 53.

24. Williams, *Christ on Trial*, 54.

25. Kevin J. Vanhoozer, "What Is Everyday Theology? How and Why Christians Should Read Culture," in *Everyday Theology: How to Read Cultural Texts and Interpret Trends*, ed. Kevin J. Vanhoozer, Charles A. Anderson, and Michael J. Sleasman (Grand Rapids: Baker Academic, 2007), 35.

26. What follows is an adapted version of Vanhoozer's strategy (see "What Is Everyday Theology?," 15–62).

27. Roy Anker, *Catching Light*, 5.

Chapter 4

1. Juhani Pallasmaa, *The Eyes of the Skin: Architecture and the Senses*, 3rd ed. (London: John Wiley & Sons, 2012), 71.

2. Paul Ricoeur, *Hermeneutics and the Human Sciences: Essays on Language, Action and Interpretation*, ed. and trans. John B. Thompson (Cambridge: Cambridge University Press, 2016), 145.

3. "Yo-Yo Ma, A Life Led with Bach," interview by Mary Louise Kelly, NPR Music Tiny Desk Concert, August 17, 2018, in *All Things Considered*, MP3 audio, 7:58, https://www.npr.org/2018/08/17/639571356/yo-yo-ma-a-life-led-with-bach.

4. This schema is similar to the one proposed by Charles Taylor, *Sources of the Self: The Making of the Modern Identity* (Cambridge: Cambridge University Press, 1989).

5. Hugo Ball, *Schriften zum Theater, zur Kunst und Philosophie*, http://www.textlog.de/39027.html, quoted in Philipp Blom, *Fracture: Life and Culture in the West, 1918–1938* (New York: Basic Books, 2015), vii.

6. Robert Henryson, *Fables, 7: The Preaching of the Swallow*. Quoted in part by C. S. Lewis, *The Discarded Image: An Introduction to Medieval and Renaissance Literature* (Cambridge: Cambridge University Press, 1964), 112. You can read the whole poem here: www.arts.gla.ac.uk/STELLA/STARN/poetry/HENRYSON/fables/swallow.htm. I'm grateful to Bo Helmich for putting me onto Lewis's wonderful introduction to medieval thought, especially chapter 7.

7. See John Milbank, *Theology and Social Theory: Beyond Secular Reason*, 2nd ed.

(Hoboken, NJ: Wiley-Blackwell, 2006); Charles Taylor, *A Secular Age* (Harvard: Belknap, 2007).

8. See W. David Buschart and Kent Eilers, *Theology as Retrieval: Receiving the Past, Renewing the Church* (Downers Grove, IL: InterVarsity Press, 2015), chap. 6.

9. See James K. A. Smith, *Desiring the Kingdom: Worship, Worldview, and Cultural Formation* (Grand Rapids: Baker Academic, 2009).

10. Mahlon Smith argues that theology's primary role prior to the Enlightenment was to clarify the church's shared worship. Mahlon H. Smith III, *And Taking Bread . . . : Cerularius and the Azyme Controversy of 1054* (Paris: Beauchesne, 1978), 29), quoted in Herman J. Selderhuis, ed., *Psalms 1–72*, Reformation Commentary on Scripture 7 (Downers Grove, IL: InterVarsity Press, 2015), lii n. 57.

11. For the sake of space, I condense much of the story. For more detail and nuance, see Perry L. Glanzer, Nathan F. Alleman, and Todd C. Ream, *Restoring the Soul of the University: Unifying Christian Higher Education in a Fragmented Age* (Downers Grove, IL: InterVarsity Press, 2017), chap. 1.

12. See Thomas Aquinas, *The Summa Theologica of St. Thomas Aquinas*, trans. Fathers of the English Dominican Province, rev. ed. (London: Burns, Oates, & Washbourne, 1920), I.1.2.

13. See Thomas Albert Howard, *Protestant Theology and the Making of the Modern German University* (Oxford: Oxford University Press, 2006); Edward Farley, *Theologia: The Fragmentation and Unity of Theological Education* (Minneapolis: Fortress, 1994).

14. Brian E. Daley, foreword to *Saving Wisdom: Theology in the Christian University*, by Brian W. Hughes (Eugene, OR: Wipf & Stock, 2011), x.

15. For Augustine, the fear of God and Christian holiness precedes the pursuit of knowledge (*On Christian Teaching* 2.16).

16. Quoted in Howard, *Protestant Theology*, 17.

17. On the latter approach, see for instance John Webster and Stanley Hauerwas. Webster, *God without Measure: Working Papers in Christian Theology*, vols. 1 and 2 (London: T&T Clark, 2018); Hauerwas, *The State of the University: Academic Knowledges and the Knowledge of God* (Hoboken, NJ: Wiley-Blackwell, 2007).

18. See Rowan Williams, prologue to *On Christian Theology* (Hoboken, NJ: Wiley-Blackwell, 2000), xii–xvi.

19. Ola Sigurdson, *Heavenly Bodies: Incarnation, the Gaze, and Embodiment in Christian Theology* (Grand Rapids: Eerdmans, 2016), 31–37.

20. Eberhard Jüngel, *Theological Essays II*, trans. Arnold Neufeldt-Fast and J. B. Webster (London: T&T Clark, 2014), 121.

21. C. S. Lewis, "Historicism," in *God, History and Historians*, ed. C. T. McIntyre (New York: Oxford University Press, 1977), 229, quoted in Gordon L. Heath, *Doing*

Church History: A User-Friendly Introduction to Researching the History of Christianity (Toronto: Clements, 2008), 42.

22. Rowan Williams, *Why Study the Past? The Quest for the Historical Church* (Grand Rapids: Eerdmans, 2005), 27.

23. Ian McFarland, "Heresy," in *The Cambridge Dictionary of Christian Theology* (Cambridge: Cambridge University Press, 2014), 209.

24. Ben Quash and Michael Ward, eds., *Heresies and How to Avoid Them: Why It Matters What Christians Believe* (Grand Rapids: Baker Academic, 2007), 1. For Roman Catholic Christians, heresy is defined even more broadly to include anyone who denies a teaching that the Roman Church has defined as "dogma" by official papal decree.

25. The Christian Reformed Church addressed the complexities involved with defining a heresy in a theologically nuanced and pastoral way at their 2020 Synod. See "What Is Heresy? Synod 2019 Asked; Report Tried to Answer," *The Banner*, June 2021, https://www.crcna.org/sites/default/files/2020_agenda.pdf, 68–77.

26. Anselm, *De incarnatione*, quoted in Douglas Farrow, *Theological Negotiations: Proposals in Soteriology and Anthropology* (Grand Rapids: Baker Academic, 2018), 172.

27. Pardon the long note, but this is an important question: When does false belief invalidate authentic faith? Could it be that when reading a heretic I'm not actually reading a Christian? Yes, that's possible, but nonetheless I believe we should read them *as if* we are siblings in Christ. I have three reasons for this. First, only God knows the content of our belief at the depth of our innermost selves. Some have confessed Christ and not been Christians (see Matt. 10 and Mark 9), speaking the truth without believing a word of it. Thus, I resist judging the authenticity of someone's faith. Second, Jesus says that the community of his disciples will always include "wheat" and "weeds" (Matt. 13:24–30). By "wheat" he means authentic disciples and by "weeds" he means false ones. The point is that God knows the difference, and *God* will separate them in the end. Thus, while I will participate in discerning true and false Christian teaching, I am wary to do here and now what Jesus said God will do in the future: judge the authenticity of someone's faith. Third, I am increasingly conscious that while our knowledge of God may be true, it is always partial. We should seek to believe and live rightly, in conformity to God's revealed truth, but our theology is "ectypal." That is, we cannot know God as God knows God (see chapter 2). Thus, toward those who believe and teach falsehoods that they sincerely believe are true, I seek to be generous. Though I will not bless their stubbornness when the Christian community corrects them, I still read them as a sibling in Christ seeking to know God and everything in light of God. When

does false belief invalidate authentic faith? I do not know, but I trust that God knows and will separate the weeds from the wheat at the time of his choosing.

28. Irenaeus, *Against Heresies*, trans. Alexander Roberts and William Rambaut, in vol. 1 of *Ante-Nicene Fathers*, ed. Alexander Roberts, James Donaldson, and A. Cleveland Coxe (Buffalo, NY: Christian Literature Publishing Co., 1885), 3.6.4.

29. David I. Smith, *Learning from the Stranger: Christian Faith and Cultural Diversity* (Grand Rapids: Eerdmans, 2009), 118, 120.

Chapter 5

1. Steen Eiler Rasmussen, *Experiencing Architecture* (Cambridge, MA: MIT Press, 1962), 10.

2. John Behr, "A Feast of Theology," in *Holy Week: A Series of Meditations* (Yonkers, NY: St. Vladimir's Seminary Press, 2018), 171.

3. Timothy Gorringe, *Discerning Spirit: A Theology of Revelation* (Philadelphia: Trinity Press International, 1990), 6.

4. Karl Barth, *Church Dogmatics*, I/2, *The Doctrine of the Word of God*, trans. G. T. Thomson and Harold Knight, ed. G. W. Bromiley and T. F. Torrance (New York: T&T Clark, 2009), 1.

5. Thomas Oden, *Systematic Theology*, vol. 1 (Peabody, MA: Hendrickson, 2006), 342.

6. Karl Barth, *Deliverance to the Captives* (Eugene, OR: Wipf & Stock, 2010), 44. Emphasis added. Barth has more to say about this in his unfinished, fourteen-volume *Church Dogmatics*, III/3, 424. Robert Jenson says nearly the same: "So, spatially, where is heaven? I answer: wherever God is. . . . When God comes to us, he comes from where he wants to bring us. And that 'from' is heaven." Robert Jenson, *A Theology in Outline: Can These Bones Live?*, ed. Adam Eitel (Oxford: Oxford University Press, 2016), 37–38.

7. You might be thinking about Jesus's ascension, which makes us think "up," especially since the apostles report seeing him go "up" into the clouds. I will say two things about this. First, the whole point of "ascension" language is Jesus's movement into royal authority. Kings ascend the throne. Jesus's going up is the visual demonstration of his ascension to the Father's right hand, not up so much as *into* authority. See Acts 1:9–11. There are clues to the spatiality of heaven in Jesus's teaching about prayer. Jesus teaches us to pray that God's kingdom would come *here*, among us as it is in heaven: "May your kingdom come, your will be done, on earth as it is in heaven" (Matt. 6:10). In heaven, God's rule is completely established, so Jesus teaches we should pray for that state of affairs to be true here also, among us. "May God rule here among us as he does in heaven. May his will

be perfectly executed as it is in heaven." In all the places we long for wholeness and healing, we should pray for the kingdom's presence – for what is true in heaven to be true there in that place where we pray for it to be so. Second, prior to Copernicus, earth was thought to be the center of seven heavenly spheres, with the "uppermost" one being where God dwells, namely heaven. Thus, going up into the clouds didn't throw off medieval Christians because it fit their cosmology.

8. In the sentences that follow I offer an extremely compressed account of God's relation to the world in which any kind of stark contrast or rival relationship between divine and non-divine agency is firmly rejected, without transgressing (of course) the ontological distinction between God and creation. I take this to be a basic assumption in theology, woven throughout the Christian tradition, but it may not be so for every reader. I recommend the following: Robert Barron, *The Priority of Christ: Toward a Postliberal Catholicism* (Grand Rapids: Baker Academic, 2007), chaps. 11–14; Kent Eilers, *Faithful to Save: Pannenberg on God's Reconciling Action* (London: T&T Clark, 2011), chap. 1; William C. Placher, *The Domestication of Transcendence: How Modern Thinking about God Went Wrong* (Louisville: Westminster John Knox, 1996); Kathryn Tanner, *God and Creation in Christian Theology: Tyranny or Empowerment?* (Minneapolis: Fortress, 1988), chap. 2; John Webster, *God without Measure: Working Papers in Christian Theology*, vol. 1 (London: T&T Clark, 2016), chaps. 8 and 9; Rowan Williams, *Christ the Heart of Creation* (London: Bloomsbury, 2018), 1–35, 169–218.

9. Sometimes called the "Wesleyan Quadrilateral," these four sources can't be attributed to John Wesley himself: see Ted Campbell, "The 'Wesleyan Quadrilateral': The Story of a Modern Methodist Myth," *Methodist History* 29, no. 2 (January 1991): 87–95. Rather, we see the interplay of these four sources throughout the history of Christian thought going back as early as Origen of Alexandria's *On First Principles* (third century). It is not a stretch to say that we find them present even in the teachings of Jesus and Paul in the documents of the New Testament.

10. "Believe, teach, and profess" is Jaroslav Pelikan's phrase. See Pelikan, *The Christian Tradition: A History of the Development of Doctrine*, vol. 1, *The Emergence of the Catholic Tradition (100-600)* (Chicago: University of Chicago Press, 1975), 1. I adapt the following subheadings, such as "The Word Remembered," from Thomas Oden's *Systematic Theology*, 3:330–51.

11. The "word of the Lord," which the author of Hebrews says is "alive and active" (Heb. 4:12), is not, in this case, Scripture, but rather the gospel message *through which* Christ *himself* is living and active. See Herman Bavinck, *Reformed Dogmatics*, vol. 1 (Grand Rapids: Baker Academic, 2003), 253–55, 380–81, 402. Thus, near the end of the letter, the author warns, "See to it that you do not refuse *him who speaks*" (Heb. 12:25). The living and active word of the Lord is *Christ*

himself, who uses the gospel message, and by extension the Scriptures which bear witness to it, to make himself present. Paul frequently refers to the gospel as Christ himself (Rom. 5:15–17; 1 Cor. 4:7; Col. 1:25–28; 3:16; Gal. 1:16), and in some cases proclaiming the gospel and "preaching Christ" appear synonymous (1 Cor. 1:17, 23; 1 Cor. 15:1, 11–12; 2 Cor. 4:3, 4). In short: "God's penetrating and discerning presence comes to his people through his word." J. Scott Duvall and J. Daniel Hays, *God's Relational Presence: The Cohesive Center of Biblical Theology* (Grand Rapids: Baker Academic, 2019), 263 (also 223–24). See also Timothy Ward, *Words of Life: Scripture as the Living and Active Word of God* (Downers Grove, IL: InterVarsity Press, 2009), 65–73. Holy Scripture is neither *inert* nor *itself* living and active; it does not have its own agency. Rather, Scripture is the written bearer of the gospel message that Christ gave to the apostles, and through it God's revelatory presence comes near. The agency of the gospel message, carried in Scripture, lies with the *living and active Christ* who speaks by the Holy Spirit (and praise God, otherwise all hope is lost).

12. This definition was adapted from Donald K. McKim, *The Westminster Dictionary of Theological Terms,* 2nd ed. (Louisville: Westminster John Knox, 2014).

13. This definition was inspired by Ellen Charry, "Experience," in John B. Webster, Kathryn Tanner, and Iain Torrance, eds., *Oxford Handbook of Systematic Theology* (Oxford: Oxford University Press, 2009), 413–31.

14. Eugene Peterson, *A Long Obedience in the Same Direction: Discipleship in an Instant Society* (Downers Grove, IL: InterVarsity Press, 2000).

15. Theologians across many different Christian traditions are presently retrieving the resources of the spiritual perception tradition. See Paul L. Gavrilyuk, "Discerning God's Mysterious Presence: Towards a Retrieval of the Spiritual Senses Tradition" (paper, Annual Meeting of the American Academy of Religion, San Diego, CA, November 22, 2014); Sarah Coakley and Paul L. Gavrilyuk, eds., *The Spiritual Senses: Perceiving God in Western Christianity* (Cambridge: Cambridge University Press, 2012); Sarah Coakley, *God, Sexuality, and the Self: An Essay "On the Trinity"* (Cambridge: Cambridge University Press, 2013), especially 88–89; Interviews with theologians working to retrieve this tradition can be watched at the website of *The Spiritual Perception Project*, hosted by Paul L. Gavrilyuk, https://spiritualperceptionproject.wordpress.com/.

16. John Wesley, "An Earnest Appeal to Men of Reason and Religion," in *The Works of John Wesley*, ed. Gerald Cragg, vol. 11 (Nashville: Abingdon, 1987), 57.

17. A. W. Tozer, *The Pursuit of God: The Human Thirst for the Divine* (Camp Hill, PA: Christian Publications, 1993), 90.

18. "Spiritual Perception & Contemporary Theology with Sarah Coakley," interview by Mark McInroy, Spiritual Perception Program, video, 24:41, https://

paulgavrilyuk.wordpress.com/projects/spiritual-perception/. See also Coakley, *God, Sexuality, and the Self*, 43.

19. A. N. Williams argues that all theology is "systematic" on the grounds that it attempts to trace the internal connections of Christian thought. A. N. Williams, *The Architecture of Theology: Structure, System, and Ratio* (Oxford: Oxford University Press, 2011).

20. Oden, *Systematic Theology*, 1:339. Emphasis added.

21. See Kevin J. Vanhoozer, Charles A. Anderson, and Michael J. Sleasman, eds., *Everyday Theology: How to Read Cultural Texts and Interpret Trends* (Grand Rapids: Baker Academic, 2007); Clifford Geertz, *The Interpretation of Cultures* (New York: Basic Books, 1973), 89.

22. Robert K. Johnston, *God's Wider Presence: Reconsidering General Revelation* (Grand Rapids: Eerdmans, 2014), 199.

23. Kutter Callaway, Fuller Studio, https://fullerstudio.fuller.edu/contributor/kutter-callaway/. See also Kutter Callaway and Dean Batali, *Watching TV Religiously: Television and Theology in Dialogue* (Grand Rapids: Baker Academic, 2016).

24. I reflect on this at length in this essay: Kent Eilers, "Rowan Williams and Christian Language: Mystery, Disruption, and Rebirth," *Christianity and Literature* 61, no. 1 (Autumn 2011): 19–31.

25. Michael F. Bird, *Evangelical Theology: A Biblical and Systematic Introduction* (Grand Rapids: Zondervan, 2013), 76.

26. See Richard J. Mouw, *He Shines in All That's Fair: Culture and Common Grace* (Grand Rapids: Eerdmans, 2002).

27. John Calvin, *Institutes of the Christian Religion* (Philadelphia: Westminster, 1960), 43. He goes on: "Men of sound judgment will always be sure that a sense of divinity which can never be effaced is engraved upon men's minds. Indeed, the perversity of the impious, who though they struggle furiously are unable to extricate themselves from the fear of God, is abundant testimony that this conviction, namely, that there is some God, is naturally inborn in all, and is fixed deep within, as it were in the very marrow" (45–46).

28. Rowan Williams, *Headwaters* (Santa Barbara, CA: Perpetua, 2008), 21.

29. Charry, "Experience," 429.

30. Oden, *Systematic Theology*, 1:336.

31. For more on this principle, see W. David Buschart and Kent D. Eilers, *Theology as Retrieval: Receiving the Past, Renewing the Church* (Downers Grove, IL: InterVarsity Press, 2015).

32. Oden, *Systematic Theology*, 1:330.

Chapter 6

1. Juhani Pallasmaa, *The Eyes of the Skin: Architecture and the Senses*, 3rd ed. (London: John Wiley & Sons, 2012), 54.

2. This splintering is beautifully chronicled in Edward Farley, *Theologia: The Fragmentation and Unity of Theological Education* (Minneapolis: Fortress, 1994).

3. To gain a sense for the spectrum of approaches, see Edward W. Klink III and Darian R. Lockett, *Understanding Biblical Theology: A Comparison of Theory and Practice* (Grand Rapids: Zondervan, 2012); Richard N. Soulen and R. Kendall Soulen, "Biblical Theology," in *Handbook of Biblical Criticism*, ed. Richard N. Soulen and R. Kendall Soulen, 4th ed. (Louisville: Westminster John Knox, 2011), 26–27.

4. Michael Horton, "Historical Theology," in *Dictionary for Theological Interpretation of the Bible*, ed. Kevin J. Vanhoozer, Craig G. Bartholomew, Daniel J. Treier, and N. T. Wright (Grand Rapids: Baker Academic, 2005), 293.

5. See for instance, respectively, Lewis Ayres, *Nicaea and Its Legacy: An Approach to Fourth-Century Trinitarian Theology* (Oxford: Oxford University Press, 2004); Carl Beckwith, *Hilary of Poitiers on the Trinity: From "De Fide" to "De Trinitate"* (Oxford: Oxford University Press, 2009); Karl Barth, *Protestant Theology in the Nineteenth Century* (Grand Rapids: Eerdmans, 2002).

6. Geerhardus Vos, *Biblical Theology: Old and New Testaments* (Grand Rapids: Eerdmans, 1948), 16.

7. John Swinton, *From Bedlam to Shalom: Towards a Practical Theology of Human Nature, Interpersonal Relationships, and Mental Health Care* (Bern: Peter Lang, 2000), 7.

8. The mission of God is especially apparent in Ray Anderson's portrayal of practical theology in *The Shape of Practical Theology: Empowering Ministry with Theological Praxis*, especially chapters 1, 2, and 3 (Downers Grove, IL: IVP Academic, 2001).

9. See Daniel Hill and Daniel J. Treier, "Philosophy," in Vanhoozer, Bartholomew, Treier, and Wright, *Dictionary for Theological Interpretation of the Bible*, 591–94.

10. See Gerald Heistand and Todd Wilson, *The Pastor Theologian: Resurrecting an Ancient Vision* (Grand Rapids: Zondervan, 2015), chaps. 1–3.

11. David F. Ford with Rachel Muers, eds., *The Modern Theologians: An Introduction to Christian Theology since 1918*, 3rd ed. (Hoboken, NJ: Wiley-Blackwell, 2005), 429.

12. Peter Gilbert, introduction to *On God and Man: The Theological Poetry of St. Gregory of Nazianzus*, by Gregory of Nazianzus (Yonkers, NY: St. Vladimir's Seminary Press, 2001).

13. Ben Myers, "Theological Education: What Is It For?," *Faith and Theology* (blog), February 4, 2010, https://www.faith-theology.com/2010/02/theological-education-what-is-it-for.html.

14. Friedrich Schleiermacher, *The Christian Faith*, ed. and trans. H. R. Mackintosh and J. S. Stewart (Edinburgh: T&T Clark, 1960), 739.

15. Michael Horton, *The Christian Faith: A Systematic Theology for Pilgrims on the Way* (Grand Rapids: Zondervan, 2011), 17.

16. Horton, *Christian Faith*, 273.

17. David W. Congdon, "The Comforter: Bulgakov on the Holy Spirit," *The Fire and the Rose* (blog), October 11, 2008, https://fireandrose.blogspot.com/2008/10/comforter-bulgakov-on-holy-spirit.html.

18. Avi Friedman, *A View from the Porch: Rethinking Home and Community Design* (Montreal: Véhicule, 2015), 116.

19. Pallasmaa, *The Eyes of the Skin*, 54.

20. You might be skeptical about email's potential as a form of theology, and you wouldn't be off base; but before you write it off entirely, consider the example of psychologist and spiritual director David Benner, who offers spiritual companionship through email. It is remarkable. See David G. Benner, *Sacred Companions: The Gift of Spiritual Friendship and Direction* (Downers Grove, IL: InterVarsity Press, 2002).

21. Vincent of Lérins, *Commonitorium*, in Roland Demeulenaere, ed., *Corpus Christianorum: Series Latina*, vol. 64 (1985), 127–95. English translation available in *Nicene and Post-Nicene Fathers*, Series 2, ed. Philip Schaff and Henry Wace, trans. C. A. Heurtley (Grand Rapids: Eerdmans, 1978), 11:131–56 (available online here: http://www.ccel.org/ccel/schaff/npnf211.iii.html).

22. Philip Reinders, *Seeking God's Face: Praying with the Bible Through the Year* (Grand Rapids: Faith Alive Christian Resources, 2013), 21.

23. Hildegard of Bingen, "Who Is the Trinity?," in Gabriele Uhlein, ed., *Meditations with Hildegard of Bingen* (Rochester, VT: Bear and Company, 1983), 28.

24. Anne Lamott, *Traveling Mercies: Some Thoughts on Faith* (New York: Anchor Books, 1999), 3.

25. Thomas Oden, *A Change of Heart: A Personal and Theological Memoir* (Downers Grove, IL: InterVarsity Press, 2014), 138–39.

26. I give extended attention to the theological import of these invented worlds in Kent Eilers, "The Beauty and Strangeness of Being: Imagining God in Marilynne Robinson's *Lila*," *Crux: A Journal of Christian Thought and Opinion* 52, nos. 3–4 (Fall/Winter 2016): 60–68.

27. See Richard Viladesau, *The Beauty of the Cross: The Passion of Christ in Theology and the Arts from the Catacombs to the Eve of the Renaissance* (Oxford: Oxford

University Press, 2006); Richard Viladesau, *The Triumph of the Cross: The Passion of Christ in Theology and the Arts from the Renaissance to the Counter-Reformation* (Oxford: Oxford University Press, 2008); Richard Viladesau, *The Folly of the Cross: The Passion of the Christ in Theology and the Arts — Early Modernity* (Oxford: Oxford University Press, 2018).

28. See Rowan Williams, prologue to *On Christian Theology* (Hoboken, NJ: Wiley-Blackwell, 2000), xii–xvi. I have written on this elsewhere at length: Kent Eilers, "Rowan Williams and Christian Language: Mystery, Disruption, and Rebirth," *Christianity and Literature* 61, no. 1 (Autumn 2011): 19–32.

29. Horton, *Christian Faith*, 22.

30. Horton, *Christian Faith*, xiv.

31. For a contemporary example, consider Miguel A. De La Torre, *Liberating Jonah: Forming an Ethics of Reconciliation* (Maryknoll, NY: Orbis, 2007), or De La Torre, *Burying White Privilege: Resurrecting a Badass Christianity* (Grand Rapids: Eerdmans, 2018).

32. See Andrew F. Walls, "The Gospel as Prisoner and Liberator of Culture," in *The Missionary Movement in Christian History: Studies in the Transmission of Faith*, ed. Andrew F. Walls (Maryknoll, NY: Orbis, 1996), 3–15.

33. De La Torre, *Burying White Privilege*; Soong-Chan Rah, *Prophetic Lament: A Call of Justice in Troubled Times* (Downers Grove: IVP Books, 2015); William Placher, *Domesticating Transcendence: How Modern Thinking about God Went Wrong* (Louisville: Westminster John Knox, 1996); Sarah Coakley, *God, Sexuality, and the Self: An Essay "On the Trinity"* (Cambridge: Cambridge University Press, 2013).

34. Williams, prologue to *On Christian Theology*, xv.

35. Hilary of Poitiers, *On the Trinity*, in *St. Hilary of Poitiers: Select Works*, ed. W. Sanday, trans. E. W. Watson and L. Pullan, vol. 2 of *Nicene and Post-Nicene Fathers of the Christian Church*, ed. Philip Schaff and Henry Wace (Grand Rapids: Eerdmans, 1898), 53–54.

36. Lament psalms for the community include the following: 12, 44, 58, 60, 74, 79, 80, 83, 85, 89, 90, 94, 123, 126, 129. These are lament psalms for the individual: 3, 4, 5, 7, 9–10, 13, 14, 17, 22, 25, 26, 27, 28, 31, 36, 39, 40:12–17, 41, 42–43, 52, 53, 54, 55, 56, 57, 59, 61, 64, 70, 71, 77, 86, 89, 120, 139, 141, 142.

37. J. Todd Billings, *Rejoicing in Lament: Wrestling with Incurable Cancer and Life in Christ* (Grand Rapids: Baker Academic, 2015), 43.

38. Rowan Williams, *Christ on Trial: How the Gospel Unsettles Our Judgement* (Grand Rapids: Eerdmans, 2003), 70. Emphasis added.

39. Myers, "Theological Education: What Is It For?"

Chapter 7

1. Alain de Botton, *The Architecture of Happiness* (London: Hamish Hamilton, 2006), 71.

2. Paul Ricoeur, *Interpretation Theory: Discourse and the Surplus of Meaning* (Fort Worth: Texas Christian University Press, 1976), 88.

3. You may be wondering, Why does the city of John's vision have a wall (Rev. 21)? Given the symbolic nature of the book of Revelation, there are various ways to interpret what the wall signifies. Let me suggest that the wall in John's vision symbolizes the full inclusion of God's people rather than the exclusion of others. Doesn't this explain why the doors of this city *never close*?

4. Paul Ricoeur, *Hermeneutics and the Human Sciences: Essays on Language, Action and Interpretation*, ed. and trans. John B. Thompson (Cambridge: Cambridge University Press, 2016), 177. I am working with the difference that Ricoeur explains between "sense" and "reference."

5. I disagree with Ricoeur at this point and follow Vanhoozer and Wolterstorff. See Kevin J. Vanhoozer, *Is There Meaning in the Text? The Bible, the Reader, and the Morality of Literary Knowledge* (Grand Rapids: Zondervan, 1980), 108–9; Nicholas Wolterstorff, *Divine Discourse: Philosophical Reflections on the Claim That God Speaks* (Cambridge: Cambridge University Press, 1995).

6. C. S. Lewis, *An Experiment in Criticism* (Cambridge: Cambridge University Press, 2012), 137, 14.

7. A place to see this very clearly is John Swinton, "Who Is the God We Worship? Theologies of Disability; Challenges and New Possibilities," *International Journal of Practical Theology* 14, no. 2 (2011): 273–307.

8. Norman Wirzba, *From Nature to Creation: A Christian Vision for Understanding and Loving Our World* (Grand Rapids: Baker Academic, 2015).

9. St. Ignatius of Antioch, "The Epistle of Ignatius to the Smyrnaeans," trans. Henry Bettenson, in *The Early Christian Fathers*, ed. and trans. Henry Bettenson (New York: Oxford University Press, 1956), 41.

10. Ignatius, "To the Smyrnaeans," chaps. 6 and 7. Revised slightly for readability.

11. Michel de Certeau, "Believing and Making People Believe," in *The Certeau Reader*, ed. Graham Ward (Oxford: Blackwell Publishers, 2000), 125, quoted in William T. Cavanaugh, *Theopolitical Imagination* (London: T&T Clark, 2002), 79.

12. See Ryan Murphy's IMDB page: https://www.imdb.com/name/nm0614682/.

13. "'I Create Worlds': 'Feud' Showrunner Ryan Murphy on Making TV," interview by Eric Deggans, March 3, 2017, in *NPR Morning Edition*, MP3 audio,

5:06, www.npr.org/2017/03/03/518128765/i-create-worlds-feud-showrunner-ryan-murphy-on-making-tv.

14. According to Thomas Aquinas, practical wisdom requires right perception, right judgment, and right execution, which are the components one sees in the wise virgins of Jesus's parable that I retell in what follows. Thomas Aquinas, *The Summa Theologica of St. Thomas Aquinas*, trans. Fathers of the English Dominican Province, rev. ed. (London: Burns, Oates, & Washbourne, 1920), II-II.47.8.

15. The word translated in Matthew's Gospel as "wise" is the Greek word *phronēsis*, which later Christians translated into Latin as *prudentia* (prudence). The kind of wisdom named *phronēsis* or *prudentia* is not theoretical wisdom but wisdom in action, or what is often called "practical wisdom."

16. Alan Jacobs, *A Theology of Reading: The Hermeneutics of Love* (Boulder, CO: Westview, 2001), 24.

17. Irenaeus, *Against Heresies*, trans. Alexander Roberts and William Rambaut, in vol. 1 of *Ante-Nicene Fathers*, ed. Alexander Roberts, James Donaldson, and A. Cleveland Coxe (Buffalo, NY: Christian Literature Publishing Co., 1885), 1.10.

18. St. Augustine, *On Christian Teaching*, trans. R. P. H. Green (Oxford: Oxford University Press, 1997), 1.36.40.

19. Jason Baehr, "Open-mindedness," in *Being Good: Christian Virtues for Everyday Life*, ed. Michael W. Austin and R. Douglas Geivett (Grand Rapids: Eerdmans, 2011), 50–51.

20. As I was putting final touches on this book, I came across a very recent book in which the authors also argue that theologians must have particular intellectual dispositions: Miroslav Volf and Matthew Croasmun, *For the Life of the World: Theology That Makes a Difference* (Grand Rapids: Brazos Press, 2019). The dispositions they outline wonderfully resonate with those I present in the following pages, as well as the "rules" I discuss later in the chapter. Volf and Croasmun suggest these: (1) love of knowledge, God, and the world; (2) love of interlocutors; (3) courage; (4) gratitude and humility; (5) firmness — and a soft touch; and (6) faithfulness (140–47).

21. Ricoeur, *Interpretation Theory*, 94.

22. See Paul Lewis, "In Defence of Aristotle on Character: Toward a Synthesis of Recent Psychology, Neuroscience and the Thought of Michael Polanyi," *Journal of Moral Education* 41, no. 2 (2012): 155–70; Timothy S. Reilly and Darcia Narvaez, "Character, Virtue, and Science: Linking Psychological and Philosophical Views," *Philosophy, Theology and the Sciences* 5, no. 1 (2018): 51–79.

23. Henri J. M. Nouwen, *Reaching Out: The Three Movements of the Spiritual Life* (New York: Image Books, 1966), 67, 71.

24. Agbonkhianmeghe E. Orabator, *Theology Brewed in an African Pot* (Maryknoll, NY: Orbis, 2008), 79.

25. Paul J. Griffiths, *Intellectual Appetite: A Theological Grammar* (Washington, DC: Catholic University of America Press, 2009), 21.

26. Griffiths, *Intellectual Appetite*, 22.

27. Simone Weil, "Letter to Joë Bousquet, 13 April 1942," in Simone Pétrement, *Simone Weil: A Life*, trans. Raymond Rosenthal (New York: Pantheon, 1976), quoted in *Oxford Essential Quotations*, ed. Susan Ratcliffe, 4th ed. (Oxford: Oxford University Press, Online Version 2016).

28. David I. Smith, *Learning from the Stranger: Christian Faith and Cultural Diversity* (Grand Rapids: Eerdmans, 2009), 119–20.

29. Jamil Zaki, *The War for Kindness: Building Empathy in a Fractured World* (New York: Crown, 2019), 178–82.

30. Zaki, *War for Kindness*, 180.

31. Zaki, *War for Kindness*, 181.

32. Lewis, *Experiment in Criticism*, 137.

33. Paul Bloom, *Against Empathy: The Case for Rational Compassion* (New York: Ecco, 2018).

34. "In 'Operation Finale,' Ben Kingsley Summons the Evil of a Holocaust Architect," interview by Rachel Martin, August 29, 2018, in *NPR Morning Edition*, MP3 audio, 7:18, www.npr.org/2018/08/29/642645179/in-operation-finale-ben-kingsley-summons-the-evil-of-a-holocaust-architect.

35. Juhani Pallasmaa, *The Embodied Image: Imagination and Imagery in Architecture* (Hoboken, NJ: Wiley, 2011), 100.

36. Lewis, *Experiment in Criticism*, 137.

37. C. S. Lewis, *The Screwtape Letters, with Screwtape Proposes a Toast* (New York: Macmillan, 1961), 183.

38. Rowan Williams, *Christ on Trial: How the Gospel Unsettles Our Judgement* (Grand Rapids: Eerdmans, 2003), 62.

39. Karl Barth, *The Göttingen Dogmatics: Instruction in the Christian Religion*, trans. G. W. Bromiley (Grand Rapids: Eerdmans, 1991), 5.